Nature Speaks
Are We Listening?

PJ Stemmler

TEACH Services, Inc.
P U B L I S H I N G
www.TEACHServices.com • (800) 367-1844

World rights reserved. This book or any portion thereof may not be copied or reproduced in any form or manner whatever, except as provided by law, without the written permission of the publisher, except by a reviewer who may quote brief passages in a review.

The author assumes full responsibility for the accuracy of all facts and quotations as cited in this book. The opinions expressed in this book are the author's personal views and interpretations, and do not necessarily reflect those of the publisher.

This book is provided with the understanding that the publisher is not engaged in giving spiritual, legal, medical, or other professional advice. If authoritative advice is needed, the reader should seek the counsel of a competent professional.

Copyright © 2016 TEACH Services, Inc.
ISBN-13: 978-1-4796-0567-5 (Paperback)
ISBN-13: 978-1-4796-0568-2 (ePub)
ISBN-13: 978-1-4796-0569-9 (Mobi)
Library of Congress Control Number: 2015914763

All scripture quotations are taken from the King James Version. Public domain.

Published by

TEACH Services, Inc.
PUBLISHING
www.TEACHServices.com • (800) 367-1844

ACKNOWLEDGEMENTS

I would like to give thanks, first of all, to God, our Creator, our Redeemer, and our Friend, for giving us His book of nature to learn from.

Second, I want to thank all those who by some way have contributed to the writing of this book, by their sharing of lessons, by their enthusiasm in learning lessons, by patience as I write, by editing, by printing, by publishing, by encouragement, by publicizing, by praying, and by learning.

May God bless everyone who reads this book with a greater hunger and thirst for Him.

TABLE OF CONTENTS

Introductory Thoughts 7

Chapter 1: Go to the Ants 9

Chapter 2: What's Buzzing? 12

Chapter 3: Our Feathered Friends 17

Chapter 4: Butterflies 21

Chapter 5: As the Deer 26

Chapter 6: Expressions of Love 30

Chapter 7: Forest Creatures 33

Chapter 8: The Blade of Grass 37

Chapter 9: Wonders in the Heavens 39

Chapter 10: The Textbook 44

Chapter 11: Rocks 48

Chapter 12: Planting Pointers 52

Chapter 13: Taught by a Fish 56

Chapter 14: Sheep Need Shepherds 59

Chapter 15: Watch the Trees Grow 64

Chapter 16: Water 67

Epilogue: More Thoughts 71

Appendix: Activities Section 72

Introductory Thoughts

You are about to enter into a study using the Lord's largest book—the book of nature. Why? The Bible teaches us that we can learn much if we will ask the beasts, the birds, and the visible things of creation to teach us about the invisible attributes of our Creator.

I remember many years ago trying to learn lessons from God's creation, but it just wasn't working. As I prayed for wisdom, ideas started to come to my mind, and I started to write them down.

My hope is that as you study and learn about His creation you will grow to know and love the Creator even more. Happy learning!

PJ

Chapter 1
Go to the Ants

"Go to the ant, thou sluggard; consider her ways, and be wise."
Proverbs 6:6

Have you heard this proverb before? Why would inspiration tell us to study such a small little bug, especially one that can be so annoying should you be trying to have a picnic or keep them out of your cupboards and food?

God does not place recommendations or commands in His Word for no reason. He has lessons for us to learn. If we read the passage carefully, we will find many principles to be incorporated or lived out in our lives.

Proverbs 6:6–11 says, "Go to the ant, thou sluggard; consider her ways, and be wise: Which having no guide, overseer, or ruler, provideth her meat in the summer, and gathereth her food in the harvest. How long wilt thou sleep, O sluggard? when wilt thou arise out of thy sleep? Yet a little sleep, a little slumber, a little folding of the hands to sleep: So shall thy poverty come as one that travelleth, and thy want as an armed man."

We can find several things about the ant within this passage:

- First it is known to be wise.
- It doesn't need someone to always be telling it what to do.

- It works hard in the summer, in the time of harvest, to prepare for hard times ahead.
- It isn't lazy.
- It will have what it needs.

The reason this instruction was given was to be of help to the sluggard. Do you know what a sluggard is? If you look it up in a dictionary, you will find that it really means someone who is lazy. As you read through the book of Proverbs, you will notice another word that is similar. It is slothful. God is not happy with laziness. How does He want us to spend our time and energy? Ephesians 5:16 states, "Redeeming the time, because the days are evil." Basically, this means that we should make the best use of our time especially because of the evil days we live in.

Did you notice that the ant didn't need someone to always tell it what to do? What can we call that characteristic? Initiative!

Be Diligent

Did you notice that the ant didn't need someone to always tell it what to do? What can we call that characteristic? Initiative! It is the ability to see what has to be done and do it, without being asked. Is this helpful? Yes, it is. The Bible reminds us that " whatsoever ye do, do it heartily, as to the Lord, and not unto men" (Col. 3:23).

When you read Proverbs 6:8 carefully, you can see that the reason the ants were so busy was to provide for the winter. Do we need to plan ahead and work to provide for the future? Reading 1 Timothy 5:8 ("But if any provide not for his own, and specially for those of his own house, he hath denied the faith, and is worse than an infidel") and Proverbs 31:21, 27, ("She is not afraid of the snow for her household: for all her household are clothed with scarlet.... She looketh well to the ways of her household, and eateth not the bread of idleness"), we find extra instruction about being prepared.

In this world in which we live, it has become quite common to do nothing. In fact, when young people are asked to work, they often complain. Is this right to do? No, it is not. God gave us work, and it is a blessing when done the right way and for the right reason. What should we remember when doing any duty? Colossians 3:23, 24 sums it up: "And whatsoever ye do, do it heartily, as to the Lord, and not unto men; Knowing that of the Lord ye shall receive the reward of the inheritance: for ye serve the Lord Christ."

I really have enjoyed reading the little that is written of the life of Christ when He was young. The Bible says of Jesus, "And the child grew, and waxed strong in spirit, filled with wisdom: and the grace of God was upon him" (Luke 2:40). We are given some encouragement to cultivate similar habits in our own lives. We find that He was raised in a carpenter's home to love and respect His parents, His neighbors, and His work. I am sure He spent his time wisely doing good deeds and completing all that needed doing.

Wow! That makes me want to work hard and to the best of my ability. What about you?

Don't Give Up!

What do you do when you are faced with some challenging task? Do you quickly give up and hope someone else will do it? Do you call for help? Or do you take a few moments to pray for wisdom and then figure out how to solve the problem?

Often, during the summer months, we enjoy picnic lunches. But, usually, where there are picnics, there are ants. I think they feel like we brought the food for them. They are quite content with crumbs, so it is not so bad. Have you ever watched a tiny ant trying to carry or pull something many times larger than itself? I have. It is a miracle to see how it keeps on trying and trying and trying.

Jesus tells us that this quality will be helpful on the way to heaven as well. Here is a special Bible verse. Galatians 6:9: "And let us not be weary in well doing: for in due season we shall reap, if we faint not." What should we remember? Don't get tired and give up!

Not giving up is called persevering. Why do we need to tell people to persevere? The way to heaven is not the easiest path. Look in Matthew 7:13, 14: "Enter ye in at the strait gate: for wide is the gate, and broad is the way, that leadeth to destruction, and many there be which go in threat: Because strait is the gate, and narrow is the way, which leadeth unto life, and few there be that find it."

Where does the easy path lead to? What about the narrow, harder path? Now, which one would you like to have? If you chose the narrow path, remember that will mean some work. Count the cost and then give it all you have to reach the goal of eternal life. It will be more than worth it. It will take lots of courage but what does God promise us? "Have not I commanded thee? Be strong and of a good courage; be not afraid, neither be thou dismayed: for the Lord thy God is with thee whithersoever thou goest" (Joshua 1:9).

So let's learn from those ants and go forward, no matter what!

Apply It!

1. Ask yourself, "Am I lazy, or do I like to work?"
2. If I am lazy, what can I do to change it?
3. Am I persevering when I want to quit? As you think about the ant, consider one job you usually complain about and choose to work diligently and cheerfully at it instead.

CHAPTER 2
WHAT'S BUZZING?

"The judgments of the LORD are true and righteous altogether. More to be desired are they than gold, yea, than much fine gold: sweeter also than honey and the honeycomb."
Psalm 19:9, 10

How many of you have ever eaten fresh honey? Did you like it? Did you wonder where it came from? Have you ever had the opportunity to find a hive of bees in the wild or to view a domestic colony? So often we are afraid of these buzzing creatures, but God made them with a purpose. Let's see what lessons we can learn from the bee in this chapter

Bees are one of God's most fascinating creatures. They work hard to bring the goodness of nectar and sweetness of honey to our tables and our taste buds. How do they work? Bees work together in their home called a hive. Different bees do different jobs to make this sweet food.

GO SEARCHING

When you see one bee or a few bees near the flowers or trees, what are they doing? They are looking for food. The sweet nectar and nutty pollen from flowers on trees and plants all serve a purpose in the beehive. But in order to find food, they must first search for it. That is where a special group of bees called "forager" bees comes in. They are sent out to look for a source of food. They fly high and low for a radius of possibly two or more miles. Why? It is their job to help the others in their colony to live, and by doing this they help themselves.

There is a lesson for us in this. There is something that each of us is to search for? Read Jeremiah 29:13 with me: "And ye shall seek me, and find me, when ye shall search for me with all your heart." Now turn to Isaiah 55:6: "Seek ye the Lord while he may be found, call ye upon him while he is near."

When the bees find nectar, they gather it and take it back to the hive to share with the rest of their colony. Can you think of what we should do when we find the Lord? In John 1:45 we have the example of one young man who found Jesus and then went and immediately told his friend the good news. "Philip findeth Nathanael, and saith unto him, We have found him, of whom Moses in the law, and the prophets, did write, Jesus of Nazareth, the son of Joseph."

Also in Luke 7:22 there is another example of what we can share with others. "Then Jesus answering said unto them, Go your way, and tell John what things ye have seen and heard; how that the blind see, the lame walk, the lepers are cleansed, the deaf hear, the dead are raised, to the poor the gospel is preached."

What if the searching seems too difficult? What can we learn from the bees? They persevere, just like the ants! Even when it is a little too cool or hot to be flying, or even if it is lightly raining, when food is scarce the bees are out. In fact, even when their honey stores are full, they are out searching wherever and whenever they can. They just cannot seem to be idle. This reminds me of something else in the Bible.

Jesus was teaching the people a lesson through the parable of the workers in the vineyard. In Matthew 20:6 He said, "And about the eleventh hour he went out, and found others standing idle, and saith unto them, Why stand ye here all the day idle?" He tells us that when the time is almost done, and when there is a great work to still be finished, some are just "hanging out," standing idle, not doing what is necessary.

One of the greatest lessons the bees teach is of united labor. They work together for a common cause.

In Matthew 7:14, we find another thought. The way that leads to eternal life follows a different path than the broad way to destruction. The broad way is easy; the narrow way takes effort. "Because strait is the gate, and narrow is the way, which leadeth unto life, and few there be that find it."

No Man Is an Island

One of the greatest lessons the bees teach is of united labor. They work together for a common cause. What does the Bible tell us about our work? Romans 15:30 says, "Now I beseech you, brethren, for the Lord Jesus Christ's sake, and for the love of the Spirit, that ye strive together with me in your prayers to God for me." We are to strive together, or be united.

Are there only some bees that work together while others do nothing? Sometimes it seems so. The drones, or the male bees, do not have an active job, but we will learn more about them later. All the female bees have their various duties, and they do them diligently. If you read 1 Corinthians 12:12–26 you will read about the many parts of the body. Are they all the same? No! Which ones are necessary and which can we do without? None! All are important. So it is in the beehive, and so it is with us. No one is more important than another. All are important to Jesus. He died for each one, and He has a special plan for your life. Will you let Him guide you?

Where can we learn to work together like the bees do in their home? Well, in our own home of course. When we are diligent to do our duties what will result? We will develop a character that will be diligent in all things. If we take the Bible instruction to do all things for the glory of God, in all our little duties and jobs at home, if we do them happily, this will help us to be able to work for Jesus in any way He asks us to.

The Center

Any beekeeper will tell you that a hive without a queen is in great danger! Why? She is the center—she is the means to create more life. When she dies, the sound of the hive actually changes from a steady hum to a "roar"!

She is their sense of security and prosperity. In the colder temperatures of winter, all of the other bees collectively work to protect her from freezing. They take turns near her to fan and warm the space around her. The bees rotate their positions so that the outside layers do not freeze. What service, what self-sacrifice!

Who is our Center, our Source of peace and prosperity? "Grace and peace be multiplied unto you through the knowledge of God, and of Jesus our Lord, According as his divine power hath given unto us all things that pertain unto life and godliness, through the knowledge of him that hath called us to glory and virtue" (2 Peter 1:2, 3). Whose directions should we be following? Our Lord's of course, for He is our Creator.

Thinking of the bees closeness to the queen, how can we be closer to Him now than we were before? John 15:14 states, "Ye are my friends, if ye do whatsoever I command you." Similarly, James 4:8 says, "Draw nigh to God, and he will draw nigh to you. Cleanse your hands, ye sinners; and purify your hearts, ye double minded." To cleanse one's hands means to do only right actions, and to purify the heart is to think only good thoughts. Doing what God wants will bring us closer to Him.

When we choose to focus on Jesus, allowing Him to be our Lord, our Guide, our Leader, we will find the truest happiness and right direction. Duties will become a pleasure even if it requires sacrifice. Our highest goal will be to do work for Christ.

When we look to Jesus the way He wants us to, then Psalm 119:103 will become our reality. "How sweet are thy words unto my taste! yea, sweeter than honey to my mouth!"

No Idler

One of the strangest concepts in my mind when it comes to studying bees is the work of the drone. He is the male bee, and his work is to be the father in the hive. But it seems that he doesn't do any work like our fathers do. He is not the one who provides the food nor cares for the baby bees or even does repair work. In fact, when winter comes and the purpose of the drone is finished, the drones are actually kicked out of the hive and they die.

It doesn't seem so kind, but there is a Bible principle found in 2 Thessalonians 3:10 that the bees exhibit. If we don't want to work, we shouldn't eat. The bees show us every fall that if the drone bee isn't going to work, he will not be able to stay in the hive and eat free food. He is kicked out of the hive and dies. It is not a pleasant thought, but it is reality. I guess we had better enjoy working.

Bees show another wonderful characteristic of God's ways. Perfect order. Have you ever wondered who taught the bees geometry? They build perfect six-sided cells that join together in their pattern. There are three different sizes to determine the outcome of the egg laid within. A small cell produces a worker bee, a medium cell produces a drone, and the largest cell is for the queen. You will find this concept of God's order in 1 Corinthians 14:40.

If there is uncleanness in the hives, the worker bees work diligently to seal up what they cannot remove and to take out anything that they can dispose of. They understand by instinct that to leave uncleanness within the hive will actually breed disease and, if not controlled, lead to death! What does God say about uncleanness in our lives? "For God hath not called us unto uncleanness, but unto holiness" (1 Thess. 4:7).

You can find a list of the works that the Bible says in Galatians 5:19–21 are "unclean." Let us ask God to help us remove these things from our lives if they are present. "Now the works of the flesh are manifest, which are these; Adultery, fornication, uncleanness, lasciviousness, idolatry, witchcraft, hatred, variance, emulations, wrath, strife, seditions, heresies, envyings, murders, drunkenness, revellings, and such like: of the which I tell you before, as I have also told you in time past, that they which do such things shall not inherit the kingdom of God."

Complete What Is Set Before You

Another interesting fact about bees is that they do that which is set before them, not by another's judgment but that which they are physically developed to do. When a bee is developed from its pupa stage, its first job is to clean its room—I mean its cell. Secondly, as it grows, it is able to become a nurse bee, feeding and caring for other larvae. After a period of time, the bee develops wax glands and now it is able to help build the cell walls, to seal the cells when they are full of honey or eggs, or to do repair work in the hive. Again, there is more maturing that happens, and then the bee starts the job of the guard bee. What must they guard against? Well, of course, intruders—other bees, insects, skunks, mice, etc.! The last job on the list of things to be done by the female worker bee is foraging. She then has quite a system of communication developed to share with her fellow workers. She is a reliable messenger just like we should be. Out she must go, day after day, week after week, until finally tired and having fulfilled her mission in life, she dies.

Is there a similar situation in our lives? Yes! Each of us has been created for a special purpose. What things should we be doing faithfully? Luke 16:10 tells us that we should do everything faithfully, even the smallest task: "He that is faithful in that which is least is faithful also in much: and he that is unjust in the least is unjust also in much."

As children and young people, when we practice being faithful in our chores, helping our mother and father, we are practicing responsibility, which will help us to accept more important duties as we get older.

Remember that even if it is only doing dishes, you can serve with a joyful heart and be a blessing to your parents. We like to eat, so we should be thankful to have dishes to clean. No matter what the job, whether it is sweeping, vacuuming, scrubbing, all need to be done by someone. Do you think your mother gets excited about doing all of her duties every day? Or do you think your dad likes getting up early and working hard all day to provide you with a home and food and clothes? Your parents do their duty out of love and care for your family. And you can model the same behavior.

Remember that Jesus didn't live for Himself, just to make His life happy. He lived to help and bless others even if He had to die. What an example! Also, remember that where we find ourselves in life will be determined by what we are capable of. So learn lots and be faithful in all.

There is a special blessing that comes when we cheerfully help those around us? That blessing is satisfaction and peace. We will not be discontented, bored, or lonely if our focus is about helping others. Try it and see.

Where do the bees get their energy from? They use pollen and nectar, and when they cannot get the fresh source of food, they use their stored resources, which we call honey. Where will we find our strength and energy to do God's will? King David reminds us in Psalm 27:1: "The Lord is my light and my salvation; whom shall I fear? the Lord is the strength of my life; of whom shall I be afraid?" Let's learn from the bees and get buzzy (busy) doing good things by God's help and strength.

Apply It!

1. Did you search out some of the words of Jesus this week so that you could learn more about Him?
2. Which duties do you need to be more faithful with in order to help your family more?
3. Did Jesus give you any directions this week through His Word or through your parents? Did you consider them sweet?
4. What can you do to have more order in your life and in your home this next week? Will you do it?
5. Make a list of the jobs you are capable of helping with. Volunteer your help to your mom or dad and watch how they react!

Chapter 3
Our Feathered Friends

"They that wait upon the LORD shall renew their strength; they shall mount up on wings as eagles."
Isaiah 40:31

Oh, to be a bird flying over the trees, the hills, the valleys, the clouds! One day, if we are faithful, we too will learn to fly in heaven. Jesus taught many lessons using the birds. Let's see what we can learn!

Neither Sow Nor Reap

Jesus taught that birds do not sow or reap. Does that mean that we shouldn't either? No, that is not what He was teaching. He had another message in mind. Let's carefully read Luke 12:24–26: "Consider the ravens: for they neither sow nor reap; which neither have storehouse nor barn; and God feedeth them: how much more are ye better than the fowls? And which of you with taking thought can add to his stature one cubit? If ye then be not able to do that thing which is least, why take ye thought for the rest?"

Jesus wanted us to realize that He cares for us, especially when we seek His will. Notice the promises in the following verses. Highlight the special words that touch your heart.

Seek ye first the kingdom of God and His righteousness; and all these things shall be added unto thee. (Matt. 6:33)

He shall dwell on high: his place of defense shall be the munitions of rocks: bread shall be given him; his waters shall be sure. (Isa. 33:16)

When we see how God cares to make His creatures beautiful, we are reminded that He will supply the needs of His children who obey Him. He promises strength, wisdom, love, patience, joy, and many other good things.

When we are concerned about something, what should we do? Philippians 4:6 says, "Be careful for nothing; but in every thing by prayer and supplication with thanksgiving let your requests be made known unto God." When we talk to God about our needs, something special happens. The next verse holds the answer: "And the peace of God, which passeth all understanding, shall keep your hearts and minds through Christ Jesus" (Phil. 4:7).

This is a much better remedy than worrying, don't you think?

Used of God

Do you think that creatures can be used to do God's work? Yes, they can! That should help us to know that each person, young or old, can also be used to do God's work, for you are of more value than any other creature. You are important!

Do you remember the story of the ravens feeding Elijah? Do you know where it is found in the Bible? Look in 1 Kings 17:6: "And the ravens brought him bread and flesh in the morning, and bread and flesh in the evening; and he drank of the brook." God used the birds to bring food to Elijah.

There is another place where we find birds helping God's people. In Genesis 8:7 we read about a bird helping Noah know when it was safe to exit the ark: "And he sent forth a raven, which went forth to and fro, until the waters were dried up from off the earth."

I see another lesson for us here. We should also be willing to be used of God no matter what He asks us to do, whether it is a small job or a large job. Just as God used birds in those two Bible stories to help others, the Bible is full of stories where God used children to do a great work. Who are some of those? Naaman's servant girl; Josiah, the boy king; Samuel, the little priest; and of course, Jesus made a difference in his home and village when He was a boy. Your name can be included too. Just ask the Lord to guide you.

Don't focus on the bad things that happen; instead, look for the blessings and praise the Lord for them.

Filled With Praise

Have you ever seen a chickadee? Do you have them where you live? They are a small black and white bird (looks like he's wearing a black cap), and he's always singing. If it is snowing, raining, cloudy, cold, or warm, he sings a song. What can we learn from this tiny creature?

The Lord is my strength and my shield; my heart trusted in him, and I am helped: therefore my heart greatly rejoiceth; and with my song will I praise him. (Ps. 28:7)

*I will bless the L*ORD *at all times:*
his praise shall continually be
in my mouth. (Ps. 34:1)

We should be like the chickadees and praise the Lord no matter what. If we will look around and think about the good blessings we see, we will find so much to be thankful for. Do you see evidences of God's love and care? Do you see plants, trees, food, people who love you, and clouds to bring rain? Do you understand that God can give you freedom from sin, salvation, and eternal life? There are so many blessings that He gives us.

So, we need to look on the bright side of life. Don't focus on the bad things that happen; instead, look for the blessings and praise the Lord for them. As you do this, the Lord will give you more blessings, more strength, and more guidance.

Connected with singing praise is an attitude that we all need. See if you can find it in Hebrews 13:5: "Let your conversation be without covetousness; and be content with such things as ye have: for he hath said, I will never leave thee, nor forsake thee." The word you should have found is contentment! We need to be joyful whether good or bad times come our way.

Here is another lesson from the birds. Have you noticed when the birds start singing and when they end? First thing in the morning, even before the sun rises, the bird choir begins to sing praises to their Maker. What should we do that is similar?

O God, thou art my God; early
will I seek thee. (Ps. 63:1)

*The Lord G*OD *hath given me the*
tongue of the learned, that I should
know how to speak a word in season
to him that is weary: he wakeneth
morning by morning, he wakeneth mine
ear to hear as the learned. (Isa. 50:4)

These verses remind us of the importance of morning and evening worship. Don't sleep in; you'll miss the best part of the day. And remember, in order to get up early enough, you need to go to bed early too. The birds show us that example as well. As soon as the sun gets close to setting, many birds find their nests, settle down, and go to sleep. So, early in the morning, and in the evening before bed, meet with your family and with your Creator, and praise Him with singing, prayer, and reading of His Word. What a wonderful idea!

Above the Trials

Where do the birds fly? On the ground, in the water? No, of course not! They fly high in the air. This reminds me of a special passage in Isaiah 40:31: "But they that wait upon the LORD shall renew their strength; they shall mount up with wings as eagles; they shall run, and not be weary; and they shall walk, and not faint."

Do you ever get weary? I do too! What does the Lord promise us if we will wait upon Him? Extra strength. This is helpful when we consider that there are many troubles in this world. When you are young, you do not face as many challenges as when you are older, but I know that in our sinful world, even children experience many disappointments and trials to bear. What do the birds do when they see trouble? They fly high. We don't have wings, but we can place our thoughts in high places, and that will help us get past the hard times.

How can we do this? Please read Philippians 4:8 and see the list of the things that we should think about, talk about, and listen to in order to help us keep our thoughts in the right place. "Finally, brethren, whatsoever things are true, whatsoever things are honest, whatsoever things are just, whatsoever things are pure, whatsoever things and lovely, whatsoever things are of good report; if there be any virtue, and if there be any praise, think on these things."

Heaven Bound

When a bird wants to fly somewhere, which direction does he head? Does he just go around in circles until he is tired? No, he has a goal, and he flies in a straight line until he reaches his destination. Have you ever heard the saying "as the crow flies" when speaking of distance? In the country it is often used to explain the shortest distance between two places. The crow doesn't allow for any distractions, bends, or stops. That's what we need to reach our goals—a straight path.

Where should you and I be heading? What should our ultimate goal be? Second Peter 3:13 tells us. "Nevertheless we, according to his promise, look for new heavens and a new earth, wherein dwelleth righteousness."

There is a special hymn that reminds me of this theme. "I'm but a stranger here, heaven is my home, earth is a desert and drear, heaven is my home." Is that where you want to go? I do. Then let us not look at this earth. Instead, let us make our decision to follow the Lord all the way home!

Once we have decided which direction we want to go, what should we do? We must keep moving; we cannot stay still. Also, we need to keep looking to Jesus as Hebrews 12:2, 3 says. "Looking unto Jesus the author and finisher of our faith; who for the joy that was set before him endured the cross, despising the shame, and is set down at the right hand of the throne of God. For consider him that endured such contradiction of sinners against himself, lest ye be wearied and faint in your minds."

Do you know the song "I Have Decided to Follow Jesus"? Have your mom or dad sing it to you or look up the lyrics. First John 2:15 tells us the same message as the song: "Love not the world, neither the things that are in the world. If any man love the world, the love of the Father is not in him." The Bible teaches us to head in only one direction—toward the cross and Jesus.

So dear friend, keep flying!

Apply It!

1. How did God help you with a concern you had this week?
2. Were you able to help someone this week and show God's love to them?
3. What are you most thankful for today?
4. What is something good, a blessing, that you can share with your friends, family, or classmates?
5. Are you ready to head for our heavenly home? Will you keep going forward and not look back?

Chapter 4
Butterflies

"Therefore if any man be in Christ, he is a new creature: old things are passed away; behold, all things are become new."
2 Corinthians 5:17

Have you seen them? Beautifully graceful, flitting in the warm breezes, landing gently on flowers, and then taking off again with the wind. They are butterflies. A beautiful creature you might think, but they weren't always so pretty. In fact, they were once a caterpillar, much like a worm. What lessons can they teach? Let's find out!

How many of you have watched caterpillars crawling along the road, a path, the wall, or your foot? Slow and steady, they don't appear to accomplish much in their lives. There are many different kinds—some are brown and fuzzy, some are striped, some are solid, some are thin, some are fat. But what is their purpose?

Caterpillars are not very exciting, nor very important in our thinking, but they, too, were created for a purpose. Let's examine the life of the caterpillar.

Each caterpillar family has a special diet. Some eat leaves from fruit trees, some from other deciduous trees, some only milkweed plants, which is the type of caterpillar I want to talk about today. Why? It's the one I am most familiar with. The monarch caterpillar is green and white and black striped. I really didn't pay much attention to them growing up, but when we saw some during our home school years, it didn't take much convincing to allow a "monarch caterpillar cage" to house many of the little "worms."

We carefully collected them and brought them to their new home, complete with their favorite meal—milkweed. The children seemed to have the right timing for collecting their specimens, for within the next day, those caterpillars got busy doing what we had hoped for. They climbed to the ceiling of their house, sent out some very fine, almost invisible silk thread and attached themselves to the ceiling where they "hung around" for awhile. I still haven't figured out how long that while is, but hang they did.

The next day as we looked, amazingly, they didn't look like upside down caterpillars anymore. They had transformed from their j-shaped hooked position to a beautiful, green chrysalis complete with a gold band around it and gold dots. Amazing! Our wonderful Creator gave them this awesome design!

I don't remember how long they hung there. We couldn't see anything happening, but obviously, something was. After what seemed like a long time, the beautiful green disappeared and was replaced with a dark color that seemed to grown blacker each day. It seemed like the skin of the chrysalis was transparent and black was within. We wondered if the monarch caterpillar had rotted inside. More patience!

Then one day, it happened. There was a crack in the cocoon. The caterpillar was trying to get out! Finally, out slipped a tiny, fuzzy, pretty creature that resembled a butterfly, sort of, but not really. It had legs, antennae, a large, very large abdomen (by proportion), and tiny wings the length of the abdomen. Suddenly, that abdomen started to pulsate. Why? It became a pump to send a liquid in its body through minuscule vessels into its tiny wings. We watched in fascination as its wings grew and its abdomen shrunk. After five or ten minutes its brand new wings were full size and gently, slowly fanning. They needed to dry out now. No flying yet, time must pass some more. The next day the roof was opened and one by one those monarch butterflies sailed away into the open air and beautiful sky to embark on a new journey.

Monarchs are known to fly from Canada (look at the map later) all the way to Mexico for their migration flight (they like the warm weather). How do they navigate all that way? The Lord who made them, built within them a special devise. The amazing part of their journey is that each monarch, should he or she survive, will come back to the place of its birth to lay eggs on milkweed plants, which will grow into caterpillars, which will turn into more butterflies. Amazing!

Now what can we learn from this process called metamorphosis? If we compare it to the life of a Christian, we can call it conversion! Step by step we can see the process that Christ wants us to experience.

First, the "worm."

The Bible teaches us that we are like a worm. "How much less man, that is a worm? and the son of man, which is a worm?" (Job 25:6). Like a worm, without Christ, we move through life without much purpose—we are consumers not producers of that which is everlasting.

Second, the fastening.

The worm reaches a point where it finds a firm source of milkweed to hold onto. It does not fasten to other plants, only milkweed. Who must we fasten onto? Only Christ. When we reach the point of wanting to be changed, we reach out by faith and grasp the promise that Christ is there to help us. This process is a big word called justification. "That being justified by his grace, we should be made heirs according to the hope of eternal life" (Titus 3:7).

> *The gold dots could symbolize His eyes that are upon us, caring, watching, and waiting for His transformation to be complete in our lives.*

Third, the cocoon.

In our illustration, I will call it a robe. When we accept Christ as our Lord and Savior, we are accepted into His family and wrapped in the robe of Christ's righteousness, not anything of our own. His righteousness is beautiful, perfect, and sinless purity. What could the green chrysalis stand for? Green is symbolic of life, freshness, and vitality. The gold line around the chrysalis is a fitting sign of the kingship of Christ. The gold dots could symbolize His eyes that are upon us, caring, watching, and waiting for His transformation to be complete in our lives.

Isaiah had this to say about God's robe of righteousness: "I will greatly rejoice in the LORD, my soul shall be joyful in my God; for he hath clothed me with the garments of salvation, he hath covered me with the robe of righteousness, as a bridegroom decketh himself with ornaments, and as a bride adorneth herself with her jewels" (Isa. 61:10).

Fourth, the waiting.

The time of waiting for the caterpillar to become a beautiful butterfly is seemingly long, much like the process of sanctification, which is the process of becoming more and more like Jesus' character every day. It is an internal work first, which means that God does His work on our heart and our thinking. Maybe no one else can see what God is doing on the inside, but the Creator knows the habits He is helping us to overcome and the attitudes He wants us to develop. He does His work quietly, secretly, steadily.

To them who by patient continuance in well doing seek for glory and honour and immortality, eternal life. (Rom. 2:7)

If a man therefore purge himself from these, he shall be a vessel unto honour, sanctified, and meet for the master's use, and prepared unto every good work. (2 Tim. 2:21)

Fifth, the hatching.

The hatching is like the trials or hard experiences that we must go through in life to strengthen us and our faith. Without them, we would die. When we go through hard times and overcome them with God's help, we are made stronger, more valiant to do the works of Christ. As James wrote, press on toward the goal: "My brethren, count it all joy when ye fall into divers temptations; Knowing this, that the trying of your faith worketh patience. But let patience have her perfect work, that ye may be perfect and entire, wanting nothing" (James 1:2–4).

Sixth, the new creature.

Finally, the new creature emerges! What a beauty! This is our goal as a Christian. This is what we are waiting for, to be beautifully recreated when Jesus comes again. We're not there yet—the job is not finished! But it is our goal to reflect Christ and to one day see our Creator face to face.

John reminds us about our character and what will happen when Jesus comes again: "He that is unjust, let him be unjust still: and he which is filthy, let him be filthy still: and he that is righteous, let him be righteous still: and he that is holy, let him be holy still. And, behold, I come quickly; and my reward is with me, to give every man according as his work shall be" (Rev. 22:11, 12).

So, what do we need to do today so that we can reach our heavenly goal?

- First, decide—"… choose you this day whom ye will serve" (Joshua 24:15)
- Second, hold on—"I beseech you therefore, brethren, by the mercies of God, that ye present your bodies a living sacrifice, holy, acceptable unto God, which is your reasonable service" (Rom. 12:1); "Prove all things; hold fast that which is good" (1 Thess. 5:21)
- Third, be transformed—"And be not conformed to this world: but be ye transformed by the renewing of your mind, that ye may prove what is that good, and acceptable, and perfect, will of God" (Rom. 12:2); "That ye put off concerning the former conversation the old man, which is corrupt according to the deceitful lusts; And be renewed in the spirit of your mind; And that ye put on the new man, which after God is created in righteousness and true holiness" (Eph. 4:22–24)
- Finally, emerge as a new creation—"Therefore if any man be in Christ, he is a new creature: old things are passed away; behold, all things are become new" (2 Cor. 5:17); "For in Christ Jesus neither circumcision availeth any thing, nor uncircumcision, but a new creature" (Gal. 6:15)

Have you begun the process? Are you being transformed? Can others see the metamorphosis in your life? Are you progressing or are you still the same person?

With some of the monarchs, they never changed. They never came out of the cocoon. They stayed the same, and we finally realized they were dead. If we live for Jesus, we will change and grow.

The Bible story of John the disciple, also known as one of the sons of thunder, shows us God's ability to change people. I imagine that John and his brother James were ones who could really speak up when they felt they needed to, hence the reason for their nickname. I also have the impression that they could get a little loud and angry about things. But the wonderful part of the story is that Jesus changed them. John wanted to be different. He spent as much time as possible near Jesus. John saw how Jesus acted, heard how He talked, thought about how He treated people, and John changed.

What about the demoniac? Do you remember how the Bible describes him? He was known to be "mad man," which doesn't mean angry, though he acted like it. Mad meant crazy. He acted as if he was a diseased animal who wanted to hurt someone. The demoniac was so strong he could break free from chains, and he scared people. But one day Jesus came to where he was and set him free. He changed. He got dressed, he talked properly, and he could think clearly. Why? Because evil spirits were no longer controlling him. In his heart, he had cried out for help, and Jesus heard him and helped him. Will He help us? For sure! If we really want to be changed from a worm to a beautiful creature, we can ask and Jesus will help us. Remember the promise: "Therefore if any man be in Christ, he is a new creature: old things are passed away; behold, all things are become new" (2 Cor. 5:17)

*A*PPLY *I*T!

1. Do you realize your need to be changed into a "new creature"? Are you tired of the old way of being?
2. Have you decided to reach out to Jesus and ask Him to change you and make you His child?
3. Memorize a Bible verse that reminds you of God's promise to change you into His image.

Chapter 5
As the Deer

"As the hart panteth after the water brooks, so panteth my soul after thee, O God."
Psalm 42:1

As you learn about God's creatures, what do you find are their basic needs? Think about cats, dogs, chipmunks, rabbits, wolves, birds, and yes, even insects, snakes, and crocodiles. They all have common needs, which if removed for a certain length of time result in death. Have you figured them out yet? Of course, food and water!

What about us? What do we need? How do you feel after a looooonnnnngggg time without food or water?

In many parts of the world, there are deer or members of that family. They have various names but similar characteristics. They are beautiful, agile, graceful, and quiet. Every time I see a deer, there is a special joy that fills my heart. How about you?

If you read Psalm 42:1, you will learn something about a hart, which is another name for the deer. What do you learn about the deer from this verse? They are thirsty. Then David compares the deer to us. What should we be thirsty for? We should long for the blessings that God alone can give.

The hart (deer) was thirsty for water. What water do we need in our lives and how often? The next verse in Psalm 42 says, "My soul thirsteth for God, for the living God: when shall I come and appear before God?"

John 4:14 tells us that we should be thirsting after the living water of eternal life that is offered through Jesus Christ. What will the living water do within us? It will make us happy! Not only that, but if we take in the living water of life, we will be like a refreshing well in a desert. The water will gush up and out of us. We will help other thirsting souls and brighten the pathway of everyone along our way.

> *It is an interesting thing with creatures that when they find water they let others know as well. They share.*

It Takes Effort

How much effort does the deer put forth to get to its water source? Where we live, you can see well-worn paths of different creatures going from the bush to the pond. What should others be able to see in our lives? Do we follow a noticeable path to the "Water of Life"?

Is it always going to be easy to get to the water? What amount of effort will be needed to get to the "Water of Life"? Jeremiah 29:13 tells us the process: "And ye shall seek me, and find me, when ye shall search for me with all your heart."

It is an interesting thing with creatures that when they find water they let others know as well. They share. We should learn how to do the same. We need to show interest, sympathy, and love to our friends and family and try to win them to Jesus.

What specific things can we do to continually drink from the fountain of living waters? Psalm 55:17 reminds us that "evening, and morning, and at noon, will I pray, and cry aloud: and he shall hear my voice."

The deer goes for its water source early in the morning just as the sun is rising and in the evening just before the sun sets. Does this sound familiar? It reminds me of when we are to meet together for worship in our homes. If we will search our hearts for wrong and ask forgiveness of anyone we have treated badly, we can have unity within our homes as we meet together and worship God. Then we can be filled with His love.

Listen Carefully

Have you ever been out hiking and managed to sneak up on a deer or a group of deer? How long were you able to watch them before they noticed you and quickly left? Do you remember the first movements the deer made? I do. The first things that moved were their ears. Why?

Deer have very sensitive hearing. They depend on their ears to protect them from danger. We need this too. Matthew 11:15 reminds us of how important it is for us to really listen. "He that hath ears to hear, let him hear."

What do we need to hear so well? We need to hear the Lord guiding us and telling us where to go: "This is the way, walk ye in it, when ye turn to the right hand, and when ye turn to the left" (Isa. 30:21).

As was already mentioned, sounds warn us. While a deer is grazing, you can notice its ears pointed upward and constantly listening for sounds. What dangers are the deer conscious of? As soon as one hears an unfamiliar crackle of sticks, the jingling of metal, or a human voice, the deer quickly moves to safety. We, too, need to be on the alert for trouble. What three dangers must we flee from?

But when he saw many of the Pharisees and Sadducees come to his baptism, he said unto them, O generation of vipers, who hath warned you to flee from the wrath to come? (Matt. 3:7)

And a stranger will they not follow, but will flee from him: for they know not the voice of strangers. (John 10:5)

Wherefore, my dearly beloved, flee from idolatry. (1 Cor. 10:14)

In the above scriptures Jesus is teaching us to flee from false teachers and being fake ourselves, from the voice or message of strangers who don't follow the Lord, and from idolatry and worshiping other things or people instead of God.

We are warned in the Bible that there will be false messengers and false messages. Unless we are connected to our Lord, we could be deceived. The Bible even warns about those who will say that they are Jesus or that they have the truth. How will we know if they are speaking the truth or not? We must study the Bible and pray every day so that we will do God's will; then we will know what is really true.

Turn, Turn!

Deer and rabbits, and even cats, have something in common. They do not head in a straight line when they run away from a noise or a bothersome creature. They run straight, then dodge right, then left, around, over, under—you get the picture! Can you guess why?

Their ability to do this is a characteristic called flexibility. They know by instinct that going in just one direction may allow the enemy to overcome them. As they change directions, they hopefully put distance between them and their predator because the predator cannot make the turns so quickly and easily, and they may even cause the animal chasing it to lose the scent of its trail.

Even though we must always be steadfast and true to the Lord and His principles, sometimes changes occur in our life according to the will of God. At these times we need to be flexible. We need to be willing to make changes. What attitude must we always keep in mind? We need to remember we are not in control—God is in control of our life.

Isaiah 64:8 reminds us that God is the designer of our life: "But now, O LORD, thou art our father; we are the clay, and thou our potter; and we all are the work of thy hand."

There are other scriptures that help us to be willing to have God shape our life:

And he said, Abba, Father, all things are possible unto thee; take away this cup from me: nevertheless not what I will, but what thou wilt. (Mark 14:36)

For that ye ought to say, If the Lord will, we shall live, and do this, or that. (James 4:15)

Are you willing to be guided and molded however the Lord wants? If so, ask Him to change you and use you to honor His name. Remember this again tomorrow and the next day and the next and the next!

Being Content

What can we learn from animals that feel unthreatened and have their basic needs met? Hebrews 13:5 (second part) and Philippians 4:11 (last part) teach us a very important lesson.

Let your conversation be without covetousness; and be content with such things as ye have: for he hath said, I will never leave thee, nor forsake thee. (Heb. 13:5)

Not that I speak in respect of want: for I have learned, in whatsoever state I am, therewith to be content. (Phil. 4:11)

We need to be c _ _ _ _ _ _! What does it mean to be content? It means to be happy and satisfied no matter what is happening or where we are.

Have you ever taken the time to watch a deer, a rabbit, a cow, or some other animal as it eats its food in the field or pen. Slowly, calmly, contently, they chew, appearing as if they don't have a care in the world. They understand the first part of Philippians 4:6: "Be careful for nothing." But we should understand and practice the second part: "But in every thing by prayer and supplication with thanksgiving let your requests be made known unto God."

Let us learn to be content while remaining alert and ready for Jesus' second coming: "Therefore be ye also ready: for in such an hour as ye think not the Son of man cometh" (Matt. 24:44).

Can you think of a young Bible character who was faithful? I can. Timothy grew up with a godly mother and grandmother who taught him lessons about God and faith, and he became a great helper to the apostle Paul and to the whole church. Wouldn't you like to be like that?

Apply It!

1. Are you thirsty for being righteous as Jesus wants you to be?
2. Have you put forth effort to make morning and evening worship interesting? Did you get enough Living Water to drink?
3. Did you practice listening carefully this week for the voice of God and the voice of your parents? They are given by God to help protect you.
4. In what way did you have to be flexible this week?
5. What do you need to be more content with? How can you do this?

Chapter 6
Expressions of Love

"Lead me in thy truth, and teach me: for thou art the God of my salvation; on thee do I wait all the day."
Psalm 25:5

As you read about the life of Jesus, you will find that He learned many, many lessons from the book of nature. How do we know? Look at how many times He taught lessons using an example from His creation.

When you love someone, you express it or show it in different ways. Some of the ways we show love are by saying "I love you," or doing kind acts for someone, or by giving them special gifts. Can you think of how you know that various people love you? God has given us some ways that He shows His love for us.

One of God's special works of art in creation is beautiful flowers. Someone has nicely written that they are expressions of God's love to us. Don't you feel His love and peace when you look carefully at the intricate design in a flower, or the clear blue of the sky, or the waving trees, or the rippling water? I am so thankful that the Lord has sent us so many messages of His love! Aren't you?

Every time we see a flower or a blade of grass or a tree, we should remember the promise of 1 John 4:8—"God is LOVE!"

Aren't you thankful for all the reminders that God gives us to show His love for us? Is there some way that you could show someone in your family or in your neighborhood that you care? Write it down and do it.

Every time we see a flower or a blade of grass or a tree, we should remember the promise of 1 John 4:8— "God is LOVE!"

Consider the Lily

When looking at flowers, have you noticed that they are not all the same? What about people, are we all the same? No! Each one is unique, special, created by God for a wonderful, special purpose. No one is less important or more important than another. Each of us can fulfill God's special plan in our lives if we will learn from the flowers.

Jesus, when He was teaching the people, pointed to one of the common flowers of His area, the lily. Though common, each particular type of flower is complex in its design. What lesson can we learn from the lily? Read Matthew 6:28–30 and see if you can figure it out. God wants to help us think of the loveliness of character that He wants each of us to have. He wants us to be like Jesus.

We spoke of the lily being common. What does God usually use to teach the greatest lessons and why? Read 1 Corinthians 1:27–29.

- God chooses foolish things
- He uses weak things
- He takes the things that are despised, even made fun of
- To confound (or confuse) the wise
- To confuse the mighty
- To bring to nothing those things which shouldn't be
- So that no one will be proud

But God hath chosen the foolish things of the world to confound the wise; and God hath chosen the weak things of the world to confound the things which are mighty; And base things of the world, and things which are despised, hath God chosen, yea, and things which are not, to bring to nought things that are: That no flesh should glory in his presence. (1 Cor. 1:27–29)

God wants us to be humble, not proud, because that is how we will learn. If we are proud and think we are strong and wise and mighty, we are not going to want to listen to our Maker. God will eventually show those people that they were wrong.

The Rose

How many of you like roses? Many people really appreciate them. What is so special about them? They are a beautiful, elegant flower that opens slowly and sheds more and more fragrance as they do.

Nature Speaks—Are We Listening?

Did you know that we can shed a fragrance in this life? Read 2 Corinthians 2:15, 16: "For we are unto God a sweet savour of Christ, in them that are saved, and in them that perish: To the one we are the savour of death unto death; and to the other the savour of life unto life. And who is sufficient for these things?"

Would you like to be a wonderful fragrance to others, giving them life and happiness? How can that happen? John 13:34 gives us the answer. We need to love one another. We need to become like Jesus.

Did you know that something else comes along with the beauty of the rose? The thorns! Look up 2 Corinthians 12:7–10. God tells us that sometimes we need to have thorns in our lives so that we learn to depend upon Him and His strength and wisdom instead of our own.

We need to remember that when God created everything in the beginning it was all very good. But sin brought sorrow and death. Sin broke the law of love and became the law of selfishness. When thorns and thistles appeared, they caused Adam and Eve to have to work. This was actually good for them and for us. When we have trials or difficulties, they are actually for our good, to help train us for heaven. Have you ever noticed that the thorny plants have beautiful flowers? Be encouraged! If you have thorns in your life, look for the roses. They are there.

There are many other lessons you can learn from flowers if you go out and look at them with an open heart. One more that comes to my mind is "to grow where you are planted." Flowers can be lovely in many places—in a nice flower bed, along the driveway, in pots in the house, in a field, and even along the side of the road. Wherever they are found, they display their beauty. What about you and me?

That reminds me of Joseph. If you don't know the Bible story of Joseph, it is a very good one to study. He was a young person who had something very bad happen to him. His brothers wanted to kill him, but instead they sent him to another country as a slave so they would never have to see him again. He tried very hard to be good and faithful there, but someone else was angry because he wouldn't do wrong and told a lie about him. He ended up in jail, but even there he asked God to help him be faithful. After a long time, he was let out of jail, and he became a strong leader in Egypt. The lesson we can learn from flowers and Joseph is to grow where you are planted. You never know what God's plans are.

Apply It!

1. Write down five ways someone has shown you love this week.
2. Think of three people and write down how they are different from you. How does that difference help you?
3. Write down five ways you can help someone in your home, then try to do it secretly.

Chapter 7
Forest Creatures

"Have not I commanded thee? Be strong and of a good courage; be not afraid, neither be thou dismayed: for the LORD thy God is with thee whithersoever thou goest."
Joshua 1:9

Have you enjoyed the challenge of learning lessons from God's creatures? Each creature is unique just like each person. Have you ever thought that you could learn something from a skunk or a porcupine? Keep reading!

He Stinketh

When you think of a skunk, what comes to mind? His cute little face, the contrasting stripes, or his fluffy tail? Probably none of those things! We usually think of his odor. But did you know that a skunk is actually quite polite?

The skunk teaches us a very important lesson described in Ezekiel 3:17. I have included the Bible verse below. The skunk teaches us the principle of warning others. He or she doesn't want to really hurt anyone. When threatened with danger, the skunk gives three warnings before spraying. First, he chatters his teeth, next he stomps his feet, and then he lifts his tail, at which point you better watch out!

Son of man, I have made thee a watchman unto the house of Israel: therefore hear the word at my mouth, and give them warning from me. (Ezek. 3:17)

It is always good to be observant, to take the warnings and change your course before having to suffer the consequences. God tells us the same thing. What does He want us to do? God wants us to turn away from evil so that we do not die. We can thank Him for the warnings, can't we? But that is not enough. We should care enough about others to warn them as well of the dangers and judgments that are coming.

Say unto them, As I live, saith the Lord God, I have no pleasure in the death of the wicked; but that the wicked turn from his way and live: turn ye, turn ye from your evil ways; for why will ye die, O house of Israel? (Ezek. 33:11)

I wonder if we really believe that the coming of Jesus is near. If we did, we would work hard to warn others to be ready. Don't you think so?

> THERE IS A SAYING THAT IS WORTHY OF REPEATING: "LEARN FROM YOUR MISTAKES, BUT BETTER YET; LEARN FROM THE MISTAKES OF OTHERS."

Do you think that something as awful as skunk spray can be helpful? Romans 8:28 says, "And we know that all things work together for good to them that love God, to them who are the called according to His purpose."

What good could come out of being sprayed? There is a saying that is worthy of repeating: "Learn from your mistakes, but better yet; learn from the mistakes of others." Being sprayed teaches a lesson not soon forgotten and, therefore, helps save you from making the same mistake twice. Can we remember that for other things as well? I think so. I wonder why so many young people make such terrible mistakes in life when others warn them of danger based on their own experience.

Let us learn from the skunk to take and give warnings before it's too late.

HE PRICKLES

Have you ever seen a walking pincushion in the forest? You know the creature I mean. He looks like floppy skin with needles sticking up, and the skin just slips and slides as he walks ever so slowly, wherever he goes.

What does Mr. Porcupine teach us? He teaches several lessons that we are going to find in the following Bible verses.

- "He that is slow to wrath is of great understanding: but he that is hasty of spirit exalteth folly" (Prov. 14:29). A porcupine is not hasty to get mad. He just slowly goes about his business, not getting upset about anything.

- "The thoughts of the diligent tend only to plenteousness; but of every one that is hasty only to want" (Prov. 21:5). A porcupine does not get in a hurry. Because they are so well protected by their quills, they are not worried about anything hurting them, so they just walk over to the nearest tree and start climbing.
- "For God hath not given us the spirit of fear; but of power, and of love, and of a sound mind" (2 Tim. 1:7). A porcupine is not afraid, at least not that I have noticed.
- "I will say of the LORD, He is my refuge and my fortress: my God; in him will I trust" (Ps. 91:2). The porcupine trusts in his God-given protection. Do we have protection too? Yes, the Lord is our safety.
- "Being confident of this very thing, that he which hath begun a good work in you will perform it until the day of Jesus Christ" (Phil. 1:6). Like the porcupine, we can be confident and walk where the Lord leads us.

Do you know what the porcupine does when an enemy approaches? He warns them and then uses those sharp arrows if they don't go away. We have a spiritual enemy—Satan. He tries to discourage us and turn us away from God. Do we have a weapon to use against this enemy of our souls? Yes, we do, and we read about it in Ephesians 6:17: "And take the helmet of salvation, and the sword of the Spirit, which is the word of God." Our weapon is the Word of God—the Bible. Do you use it?

Do you remember the story of when Jesus was tempted by Satan? We can see how He fought His enemy and how we can fight ours. We find in the Bible that He answered Satan's temptations with "It is written" and quoting Scripture. There is power in the Word of God.

There is another lesson we can learn from the porcupine. Does it ever go out without protection? Never! Neither should we. Its weapons are always attached. We, too, should have the Word of God with us at all times. We may not be able to carry a Bible everywhere and at all times, but we can carry the Word in our minds. Keep it with you always!

Just like God made each creature unique, He made each of us special, and he asks us each to do a certain work for Him. When everyone does their own specific work for God, we all blend together and help one another to follow God's master plan.

Who can you think of in the Bible that showed the same characteristics as the skunk and the porcupine? I am sure you will think of someone, but the person that comes to my mind is Noah. He warned people of the flood for 120 years. That takes courage, especially when there were so few people who believed him. But like the porcupine, he was not afraid. He knew that God was leading the way and protecting him. So be like Noah and do what God asks, no matter what happens.

Apply It!

1. Think of three times that someone warned you of danger. Are you thankful they did?

2. Think of three things that you could warn someone about and keep them from being hurt.
3. Do you have anything you are afraid of? Pray right now and ask the Lord to help you be strong and courageous.

Chapter 8
The Blade of Grass

"For a just man falleth seven times, and riseth up again."
Proverbs 24:16

How many of you have grass near where you live? There is a special characteristic shown in the humble blade of grass. How many of you have helped to cut the lawn? What happens after about a week? It needs cutting again, doesn't it? Does grass have characteristics that we should have? It sure does. When we read Proverbs 24:16, we see the principle or characteristic of persistence. It just doesn't give up and quit!

There is something else about grass that is equally important. It is the same thing that is taught in Matthew 10:31. This is to remind us that each one is valuable in God's sight. But how can grass teach us that we are valuable when we just keep mowing it down? Just think, if God gives so much attention to grass, which lives so briefly, how much more does He care for mankind whom He created? If we look carefully at the grass and flowers, the birds and trees, we find the message that God loves us.

Grass Withereth

Grass shows us the temporary nature of this life. There are many types of grass, and it may be a good project to try and find out how many varieties there are growing in the

> **WE DON'T KNOW HOW LONG WE WILL LIVE. HOW DOES THAT HELP? LIVE EACH DAY AS THOUGH IT MAY BE YOUR LAST.**

area where you live. Even though there are many types, they all will die eventually, and during a time of very hot weather or no rain, grass withers and will perish if it doesn't receive what it needs. Can this help us in our lives? Yes! It reminds us that we need the things necessary to live healthy and long, but that even with that, one day, we too will die. We don't know how long we will live. How does that help? Live each day as though it may be your last. Do right, love others, and thank God for His help and guidance. Also pray that your sins will be forgiven, and then when our time on earth is finished, we will be ready.

James tells us the following: "For the sun is no sooner risen with a burning heat, but it withereth the grass, and the flower thereof falleth, and the grace of the fashion of it perisheth: so also shall the rich man fade away in his ways" (James 1:11).

Did you know that grains like rye, barley, wheat, and oats are actually types of grasses? If left to grow to maturity, something happens to the greenness of the grass. Have you seen what occurs? It actually dies. The grain is harvested and the straw (the stem of the grass) is collected and used for bedding animals or plowed back into the ground. Its life is finished. Yet the mature grain that grew gives more life. It is made into flour and bread and cereals, which we eat to have strength and health. Isn't God good? We have a special promise from God that is linked with the short life of grass. Please read Isaiah 40:8: "The grass withereth, the flower fadeth: but the word of our God shall stand for ever." Try to remember that every time you see a blade of grass.

The apostle Paul understood the lessons from the blade of grass. He suffered a lot of persecution, but he didn't let that stop him. He grew old in the work and in the faith, but his work lives on and feeds us spiritually even today. Every time you read a great amount of the New Testament, you see something of the work of Paul

The apostle Paul had many bad experiences while being a missionary for Christ, but he wrote the following words: "We are troubled on every side, yet not distressed; we are perplexed, but not in despair; Persecuted, but not forsaken; cast down, but not destroyed" (2 Cor. 4:8, 9).

What courage! What persistence! Let us ask God for the same.

Apply It!

1. What did you learn about God's care for simple things and simple people?
2. How did you bounce back up from a trial this week like grass bounces back?
3. What lasts longer than all the flowers and grasses that we can see?

Chapter 9
Wonders in the Heavens

"And God saw every thing that he had made, and, behold, it was very good."
Genesis 1:31

As we live and move and breathe, we can see that we are surrounded by many elements, given by God, to sustain our lives and give us pleasure. As we study about the earth, we learn about the things that our Creator has given to us. When you go about your duties this week, see if you can find other lessons to share.

Don't Get in a Hurry

Even though there are so many operations or functions happening within the world of nature, we notice a wonderful thing. God is not in a hurry. He works steadfastly, thoroughly, without going so fast that mistakes are made. Can we do the same? Paul tells us in 1 Corinthians 10:31 that we should do everything for the glory of God, meaning to do all our duties in such a way that we show something about what God is like.

God wants us to be faithful, calm, and considerate, not hurried and complicated in what we do, nor careless or incomplete. God does things perfectly. He wants us to do our very best. Take some time to really look at creation. We can learn a lot if we spend some time each day in nature, or at least

> GOD IS NOT IN A HURRY. HE WORKS STEADFASTLY, THOROUGHLY, WITHOUT GOING SO FAST THAT MISTAKES ARE MADE.

each week, which is one of the reasons God gave us His special Sabbath.

Today, let's look at some interesting things in the heavens. When scientists looked at the placement of our planet, they noticed a very interesting fact. If our planet was just a little bit closer to the sun, it would burn everything upon it, including us. If the earth was just a little bit further from the sun, everything would freeze. If the earth were to spin faster or slower, what would happen? Chaos. God knew exactly what we needed and provided for our best care. Isn't it wonderful that we can trust Him with all the little and big things of life? That is why we need to pray like David, "Show me thy ways, O LORD; teach me thy paths" (Ps. 25:4).

Nothing Beneath His Notice

In the book of Job, there is an interesting account of some conversations between Job, his three friends, and finally the Lord Himself. I find it fascinating that while studying the book of Job we can read something of what God says about His creation.

In Job 38 and 39 are many nature lessons. As you read these chapters, find your favorite parts. One of the greatest things I find is that there is nothing beneath His notice. What does this mean? He sees all and knows all. If you read Psalm 139:1–16 in your Bible, you will find out that King David understood that as well. No matter what you are feeling or going through—pain, sadness, happiness, hard things, or good things—we can bring them before God in prayer and He will help you.

Laws in Motion

Sometimes when we discuss the laws of God, people think that it is not right for our Lord to have laws. They do not understand that all around us are laws—principles of cause and effect. This simply means that if you do one thing, a certain consequence will happen. For example, what will happen if you throw a ball up into the air? It comes down, right? This is a law—the law of gravity. What happens if you jump off of the side of a steep cliff? You will fall! It is the same law. No matter how hard you think you will not fall, it is a natural consequence because of gravity and the density or weight of your body. God has created our world in this way.

Can you imagine if you had no weight because of zero gravity? What would happen if you went to put on your shoes to go outside? You would have to try to catch them in the air. Now that would be tricky, because you would be floating too! What if you got thirsty and tried to get a drink of water? It wouldn't go into the glass or down your throat because gravity is what keeps all things in the right place. Aren't you thankful for gravity? I am!

God has some other laws as well. We will study one in another chapter. The law of sowing and reaping. Can you remember what it means? In the book of Job, it talks about sowing or planting iniquity, which is sin, and wickedness. Do you know what will grow or be reaped? The same things that were planted will grow. But in Hosea 10:12, we are told that if we sow righteousness, we will reap or get mercy. That's a lot better thing to receive. What do you want to grow?

There is another part to the same law. If we sow just a little, we will get just a little. If we sow lots, we will get lots. I want to reap lots of righteousness, love, and mercy. What about you? (See 2 Corinthians 9:6.)

God gave His law on Mount Sinai (the Ten Commandments) for our physical, spiritual, and mental well-being. Can you see what happens if we don't keep His laws? Sin and sorrow and suffering! Try to think of each commandment in Exodus 20 and what consequences there are when we break that law. As I look around, I see that doing what God says brings much more happiness than disobeying Him. I am thankful for all of His laws.

What About Storms?

Is every day the same where you live? Not here! Some days are sunny, some are cloudy, some have snow, some are warm, some are cold. Why are there such differences in weather where we live? Why are there storms and rain? We may not understand all the reasons, but we can have some assurance as we face life's uncertainties. What is the special promise for us? God is in control!

Even when unusual things happen, there is a reason. For instance, if you read in Job 1:9–19 about the storms that came you can learn who caused the storm, who allowed it, and why? I will leave that for you to look up for yourself.

The Bible tells us that there are some stormy times ahead, some bad things are going to happen. But there are also some special promises for us! Can you read them in Psalm 91 and 46? It is a good thing to memorize as many of these verses as you can, which is why I left the number in front of each verse.

Psalm 91:1 *He that dwelleth in the secret place of the most High shall abide under the shadow of the Almighty.*
91:2 *I will say of the Lord, He is my refuge and my fortress: my God; in him will I trust.*
91:3 *Surely he shall deliver thee from the snare of the fowler, and from the noisome pestilence.*
91:4 *He shall cover thee with his feathers, and under his wings shalt thou trust: his truth shall be thy shield and buckler.*
91:5 *Thou shalt not be afraid for the terror by night; nor for the arrow that flieth by day;*
91:6 *Nor for the pestilence that walketh in darkness; nor for the destruction that wasteth at noonday.*
91:7 *A thousand shall fall at thy side, and ten thousand at thy right hand; but it shall not come nigh thee.*
91:8 *Only with thine eyes shalt thou behold and see the reward of the wicked.*
91:9 *Because thou hast made the Lord, which is my refuge, even the most High, thy habitation;*

91:10 There shall no evil befall thee, neither shall any plague come nigh thy dwelling.
91:11 For he shall give his angels charge over thee, to keep thee in all thy ways.
91:12 They shall bear thee up in their hands, lest thou dash thy foot against a stone.
91:13 Thou shalt tread upon the lion and adder: the young lion and the dragon shalt thou trample under feet.
91:14 Because he hath set his love upon me, therefore will I deliver him: I will set him on high, because he hath known my name.
91:15 He shall call upon me, and I will answer him: I will be with him in trouble; I will deliver him, and honour him.
91:16 With long life will I satisfy him, and show him my salvation.

Psalm 46:1 To the chief Musician for the sons of Korah, A Song upon Alamoth. God is our refuge and strength, a very present help in trouble.
46:2 Therefore will not we fear, though the earth be removed, and though the mountains be carried into the midst of the sea;
46:3 Though the waters thereof roar and be troubled, though the mountains shake with the swelling thereof. Selah.
46:4 There is a river, the streams whereof shall make glad the city of God, the holy place of the tabernacles of the most High.
46:5 God is in the midst of her; she shall not be moved: God shall help her, and that right early.
46:6 The heathen raged, the kingdoms were moved: he uttered his voice, the earth melted.
46:7 The LORD of hosts is with us; the God of Jacob is our refuge. Selah.
46:8 Come, behold the works of the LORD, what desolations he hath made in the earth.
46:9 He maketh wars to cease unto the end of the earth; he breaketh the bow, and cutteth the spear in sunder; he burneth the chariot in the fire.
46:10 Be still, and know that I am God: I will be exalted among the heathen, I will be exalted in the earth.
46:11 The LORD of hosts is with us; the God of Jacob is our refuge. Selah.

There is also a promise given in 1 Corinthians 10:13 that nothing will be given to us that we cannot handle with God's help. How do the trees handle storms? Some don't! They have very shallow root systems and/or weakened trunks, and they fall. But I want you to notice the ones that stand. What are the characteristics that allow them to withstand the heavy winds, the snow, and the sun?

DAY BY DAY WE CAN GROW STRONGER AND DEEPER IN OUR RELATIONSHIP WITH JESUS. SO WATCH OUT STORMS, MY MASTER IS HOLDING ME UP!

When the winds blow, the tree gives a little. It has some flexibility so that it doesn't break. When bad things happen to us, we need to bend before the Lord, and He will give us the strength needed to stand. Those trees also have deep root systems. We can be rooted and grounded as well. Read Ephesians 3:17: "That Christ may dwell in your hearts by faith; that ye, being rooted and grounded in love." The trees all have internal systems working to give the needed nutrition and water necessary to keep everything healthy. Do we? Yes! Day by day we can grow stronger and deeper in our relationship with Jesus. So watch out storms, my Master is holding me up!

What do we need to do in order to stand firm?

- Be faithful!
- Bend on our knees in prayer.
- Be rooted and grounded in love.
- Hold on tight!

Can you think of someone in the Bible that had to go through some hard times but kept trusting in the Lord? What about Esther? She saw stormy winds when her people were all going to be destroyed, but she bent before God in prayer, along with her friends and people, and God held her firm. She stayed faithful to God, God changed the heart of the king, and her people were spared. What an example for us.

Apply It!

1. How is it possible that planets, stars, and suns do not crash into one another?
2. If God has everything perfectly timed, should we be late for things or on time?
3. What little concerns can you take to God today and let Him help you with? Pray right now about what is bothering you.
4. What laws are you most thankful for this week?
5. How can we stand firm through the storms of life?

Chapter 10
The Textbook

"The heavens declare the glory of God; and firmament showeth His handiwork."
Psalm 19:1

Have you had the awe-inspiring experience of standing under the starry skies on a very clear night? What a sight! (Of course, to get the best view you need to be far from any town or city with its artificial light.) The longer you stand gazing, the more you can see! Do the numbers of stars end? What do the heavens teach us?

The Heavens Declare ...

Have you ever wondered who stuck all those stars in the same place and pattern? Have you ever wondered whether other creatures live way out there in the heavens? Did you know that the Bible gives us that answer? What a marvelous Book!

The Bible says that the heavens show the glory of God and His handiwork (Ps. 19:1). Have you ever wondered how many heavens there are? Second Corinthians 12:2 tells us that there is a "third heaven." If there is a third, then there is a second and a first, which equals three heavens. One day, if we are faithful, we will get to see the heavens and understand all of God's creation.

If you read Hebrews 1:2 carefully you can read that the Lord made the worlds, not just the world. With so many worlds and stars and suns to care for, how does our heavenly Father view earth—the one planet stained with sin? Luke 15:4 is the parable of the lost sheep. Our world is just like that lost sheep that the shepherd left everything to go and find. Aren't you thankful that Jesus gave up everything to come rescue us?

His Glory

Glory is not a word used often in our vocabulary anymore, although in times past it was. Glory signifies something very special, very bright—something spectacular. Have you ever wondered about what the glory of God is? The glory of God is His character.

> **When we study the heavens and their beauty and complexity, we learn something of God's thoughts and feelings.**

What is character? Character is the collection of qualities or traits of a person—what they think of, how they feel, and what they do. All of this shows who they really are. How do the heavens show the character of our Father in heaven? Psalm 97:6 tells us that "the heavens declare his righteousness, and all the people see his glory."

When we study the heavens and their beauty and complexity, we learn something of God's thoughts and feelings. He must love the beautiful and be very, very wise. He has compassion for His people. He provides the direction we and the animals need through the sun and stars. He cares. He is very powerful to be able to make all of these things, and He is able to make it all work together, day after day, year after year. God is very merciful to His creation.

The Heavens Show Power

When you drive toward a city at night, what do you notice? I always notice the brightness in the sky and then more specifically all the dots of lights. Can you imagine the electricity bill needed to light up a whole city? What about the sky? How much power is needed to light it up on a starry night?

The Bible says that Jesus is the source of all light. He is the energy pack. (See John 8:12.)

Do the stars go where they want and do what they want? No, they don't. When God made them for a certain work, He gave appointed places for them. (See Job 9:7, 8 and Psalm 104:24.) We can choose to be taught by this great Creator! Wow!

How can these facts help us in our daily lives? Can God help and guide us as well? Yes, He can if we will ask and trust Him.

What About Star Pictures?

Do you like pictures? Have you studied the constellations? There are definite patterns and definite times that they appear. People called astronomers dedicate their lives to learning more about what appears in the sky at night. It would be good for us to take some time to notice these wonders in the night sky and pray that our Creator would teach us through this picture book.

Why do the stars appear in such a perfect and orderly fashion? The Bible tells us that God is a God of order. He knows how many stars there are and exactly where He placed them. (See Psalm 147:4; 1 Corinthians 14:33 (first part); 14:40.) This lesson of order will help us in our lives to want things and duties to be orderly as well. This helps life to run smoother.

Did you know that the stars, sun, and moon also teach us to be on time? What would happen if they were too early or too late? It would cause confusion and people and animals would get mixed up. The same applies to God's work for us, His purpose for our life. He doesn't make mistakes and is never late. We need to trust that He is working out the best for us in every situation.

If you find a sunset calendar and check the time of sunset this week, you will notice how accurate God is. It is interesting that scientists can even tell months and even years ahead of time when it will set. Why? Because God is always exactly on time! The same happens for the moon, the constellations, and other things in the heavens.

Have you seen a star map according to the seasons? Those who study these things know that this part of creation moves with exact timing. Can you imagine what would happen if God was late to have the sun come up or if He forgot to have the moon shine? Think about these lessons when you have duties to perform on time.

Steadfast and Unwavering

What do you notice every morning and evening? I will give you a hint. It has something to do with light. Did you guess? Every morning the sun rises and every evening the sun sets. Why? Because God made it that way (Gen. 1:16–18). What is actually happening? Scientists have noticed that the earth actually rotates around the sun. Because the earth is turning away toward the sun, it looks like the sun is moving, but it is actually our planet that is moving.

As scientists track the speed and motion of this planet and all others, they notice that the timing is very accurate. There is no deviation. Even the stars and the comets have definite patterns, and it can be projected ahead of time what movements they will make. How is this possible? Please read Job 9:4, 7–10: "He [God] is wise in heart, and mighty in strength ... Which commandeth the sun, and it riseth not; and sealeth up the stars. Which alone spreadeth out the heavens, and treadeth upon the waves of the sea. Which maketh Arcturus, Orion, and Pleiades, and the chambers of the south. Which doeth great things past finding out; yea, and wonders without number."

This Bible verse tells us who keeps the earth and all the other planets going in the same direction and the same speed all the time. It is God, our Creator.

What can we learn about God's character through these facts? We have already discussed that He is a God of order, but I want you to think about the complexity of His work. Imagine trying to keep track of an endless number of stars, planets, and other heavenly operations, not to mention the number of hairs on each head. How great is our God!

Blessings in Sunshine

Today was a beautiful sunny day! What joy sunshine brings to our hearts, and as the Bible says, it is pleasant to the eyes. Are you thankful for the sunshine? What does the sunshine teach us? It divides the day from the night (Jer. 31:35). It teaches us something about time, and also about giving. The sun gives us light and warmth every day so that plants can grow and we can thrive. Sunshine also teaches us mercy. God gives it to the just and the unjust.

The Bible compares Jesus to the sun. The sun shines on the good and the bad, giving light to all. So does Jesus. He is not picky about who He loves and who He wants to help. The sun is the source of light and warmth, just as Jesus is the source of truth and love. But what about those stars that we were talking about. Where does their light come from? Like the sun, their power is given by the Creator. We are to be like the stars and the moon and reflect the light of Jesus to others around us. How can you do that? Let Jesus fill you with His light and love, and His light will shine through.

Are there others who we can read about that were like the moon reflecting the light? What about the apostle Peter? He learned to love Jesus and went through many stormy seas in his boat. When things looked very dark, he looked to Jesus, who made the storm to stop and gave him light and peace in his heart. Wouldn't you like to have that experience too? Just ask.

Apply It!

1. How can the heavens tell us about what God is like?
2. What part of God's character is most important to you today?
3. Where does all the power of heaven come from? Did you allow Him to guide you this week?
4. What do the stars teach about being on time for appointments?
5. What does the sunshine teach us about God's great love?

Chapter 11
Rocks

"O come, let us sing unto the LORD: let us make a joyful noise to the rock of our salvation."
Psalm 95:1

I am hard. I often have designs imprinted on me. I come in different colors and shapes. I sometimes glitter and sometimes am very dull. I can be a real pain or a real help. What am I?

Unchangeable

Rock. Is there anywhere in the entire world where you cannot find this element? If you can think of any places, write them down and send the answer to me. This element seems so common and yet so important. The first characteristic that comes to mind about rock is that it doesn't change.

God is compared to rock in that He does not change (Mal. 3:6), and there is no place that He is not there (Ps. 139:7–14).

In what way can we be steadfast and unmovable? By consistently living a holy life, which means always, not just now and then. When we live for Jesus, we show others an example of who He is.

The Wise Man

Do you remember the song "The Wise Man Built His House Upon the Rock"? Have you ever wondered why he didn't use some other material? Jesus had good reasons for using this illustration. I hope you will appreciate rocks more after studying this.

The Bible teaches about the wise building on a rock because of its unchanging characteristics. In some places houses can be seen built upon rock that have stood up to storms for a thousand years, and they are still strong. However, the ones built on sand are quickly destroyed when storms and waves beat upon them.

Jesus teaches that His words are like a rock. In Matthew 24:35 He says, "Heaven and earth shall pass away, but my words shall not pass away." Isn't it wonderful to think that there is something that always remains the same, and Someone who never changes?

The Storms

Life always seems so pleasant when everything goes well. There is no danger of flooding when there is no rain, no problem with sorrow when everyone is happy. But life is not all sunshine and happiness. We can learn another important lesson from the rocks that will help us through the stormy times.

What happens to the rocks that are on the shores of bodies of water? Do they disappear when the waves get rough? How can we be like those rocks? We can stand fast in the Lord (Phil. 4:1). This is similar to being unmovable.

Instead of the rocks being removed by the rough waters, something special happens to those jagged rocks. There is a slow process of polishing that happens when water washes over rocks for long periods of time. Polishing makes a regular rock beautiful and smooth. How can we be made beautiful in character, polished? The Bible gives us the answer again in 1 Peter 1:7. It says that through "the trial of your faith, being much more precious than of gold that perisheth, though it be tried with fire, might be found unto praise and honour and glory at the appearing of Jesus Christ."

Stones of Stumbling

Years ago we used to spend many hours walking through a stone quarry, also known as a gravel pit. It was intriguing to see the various forms and colors of rock, stone, and sand. We could hike for hours over the many acres there, but we had to be very careful. Can you guess why?

What happens if you are walking, yet not watching where you are going? You will stumble and fall and maybe even get hurt. When you look in the Bible for verses about stumbling, you will find one about Jesus being a stone of stumbling (Isa. 8:14). You will also find Him referred to as another type of stone. What is it? Isaiah 28:16 refers to Jesus as a cornerstone. A cornerstone is the rock that supports the rest of the structure built around it. Why would we stumble over Jesus? First Peter 2:8 tells us the answer. If we are disobedient, we will stumble. Yet, the Bible also says we should fall on this Rock (Matt. 21:42–44). This sounds confusing doesn't it?

What Does This Mean?

I think that the following is a great definition of what it means to fall on the Rock—Jesus. It means to give up our selfishness and our sense of thinking that we are great. It means to go to Jesus as a little child, sorry for our sins and wrong doings, and believe that He will forgive us and help us live a new life.

So which would you choose—to give up sin and selfishness and be saved or reject God's love and be lost and destroyed?

How does God look at His creatures? As jewels in the rough. We haven't all been polished yet.

Hidden Gems

Some stones and rocks look very rough and even ugly to our sight, yet there may be a surprise within. What could it be? Yes, many precious gems are found within the ugliest rocks, or in the case of pearls, inside an oyster shell. When we view people, we are often apt to judge some as special and some as very rough. How does God look at His creatures? As jewels in the rough. We haven't all been polished yet.

If you read Revelation 21:19, 20 you will find quite a list of precious gems or stones. Where do they come from? From jagged rocks.

And the foundations of the wall of the city were garnished with all manner of precious stones. The first foundation was jasper; the second, sapphire; the third, a chalcedony; the fourth, an emerald; The fifth, sardonyx; the sixth, sardius; the seventh, chrysolyte; the eighth, beryl; the ninth, a topaz; the tenth, a chrysoprasus; the eleventh, a jacinth; the twelfth, an amethyst. (Rev. 21:19, 20)

Our characters are often like those jagged rocks, looking rough and unpromising, but our Lord and Creator knows that there is potential within and hidden gems to be found. If we will let Him, He will make us into a new creature (2 Cor. 5:17)!

Sometimes we look at people and think that they are unlikely to do anything well, but if others will work with them and help them, precious gems of character can be found and they will grow into what God created them to be. So don't forget to encourage others.

Many have hidden talents that no one sees. They may seem unattractive, yet the Lord can see something precious within that will stay beautiful and strong even through hard times.

What else can rocks remind us of? Read the following verses and see if you come up with anything else.

The LORD liveth; and blessed be my rock; and exalted be the God of the rock of my salvation. (2 Sam. 22:47)

He only is my rock and my salvation: he is my defence; I shall not be moved. In God is my salvation and my glory: the rock of my strength, and my refuge, is in God. (Ps. 62:6, 7)

The Lord is our:
- salvation
- defense

- strength
- refuge

I didn't think rocks could be that interesting, but when we think about them compared to God there is so much to study and learn.

Can you think of someone who stood firm with the Lord through many challenges? I think of Moses. Yes, he made some mistakes, but once He knew exactly what God wanted, he stood firm even when others turned against him. He was God's messenger to teach us about God's law, about His sanctuary, and about the whole plan of salvation given through the sanctuary service. For years Moses wandered in the wilderness, leading God's people and being a faithful follower of the Lord. What an example!

Let us help each other be firm rocks for Christ.

Apply It!

1. In what ways should you and I be like a rock?
2. How can I have the stability and steadfastness of the Rock in my life?
3. How did the Lord do some polishing in your life this week?
4. How can you submit yourself to Jesus today?

Chapter 12
Planting Pointers

"Herein is my Father glorified, that ye bear much fruit; so shall ye be my disciples."
John 15:8

Many times we have mentioned lessons from growing things. In this chapter we are going to focus on lessons just from the growing process. All of us should be able to see examples inside and outside our homes. Don't forget to share them with others.

A Time for Everything

When going about your duties day by day have you realized that there is a pattern of actions that you do or see others do? We call these routines or habits. Are they helpful? Indeed they are! Good habits and routines help us to know what to do and be prepared for the unknown and unplanned things of life. In the great book of nature, there are many examples of routines and habits. See if you can find some on your own.

If you read in Ecclesiastes 3:1–11, you will notice a very interesting collection of thoughts. How would you summarize them?

To every thing there is a season, and a time to every purpose un-der the heaven: A time to be born, and a time to die; a time to plant, and a time to pluck up that which is planted; A time to kill, and a time to heal; a time to break down, and a time to build up; A time to weep, and a time to laugh; a time to mourn, and a time to dance; A time to cast away stones, and a time to gather stones together; a time to embrace, and a time to refrain from embracing; A time to get, and a time to lose; a time to keep, and a time to cast away; A time to rend, and a time to sew; a time to keep silence, and a time to speak; A time to love, and a time to hate; a time of war, and a time of peace.... He hath made every thing beautiful in his time: also he hath set the world in their heart, so that no man can find out the work that God maketh from the beginning to the end.

There is a time for all things. Even in growing crops we have noticed the same laws. God has given certain times to do certain things, and if we try to do it at the wrong time or in the wrong place, we suffer the consequences. There is a special promise for us concerning planting and harvesting found in Genesis 8:22. It says, "While the earth remaineth, seedtime and harvest, and cold and heat, and summer and winter, and day and night shall not cease."

In gardening of any type, there is something that needs to be done before any seed can be planted. In the book of Hosea, God compares gardens with our heart and tells us to "break up the fallow ground." ("Sow to yourselves in righteousness, reap in mercy; break up your fallow ground: for it is time to seek the LORD, till he come and rain righteousness upon you" [Hosea 10:12].)

Breaking up the fallow ground means to give up the hard, lumpy parts of your character. It means putting away selfishness and disobedience. It means we need to be soft, wanting to know and to do the will of God. Will you break up your heart and make it soft for the Lord?

Not All the Same!

As seeds or plants are placed into the ground, there is something quite noticeable. Not all plants are the same. Even if you are planting all of the same variety, you will see that some are larger, some smaller, some sturdy and thick, some small and weak. Once placed in the ground, it will be found whether they are actually strong enough to survive. After some time, none of the differences are apparent. What does this teach us about people? Not all are the same.

Even as you study the different cultures of people, you find different colors, different languages, and different features. God made them all and loves them all. Does this happen in the plant world as well? Of course! God likes variety. Take some flowers of the same kind and see how many differences you notice between them. Does that make them useless or unable to do their work? No, of course not! So we can see that even though there are differences in people, they can still be useful and work together to honor God and bless humanity. In Romans 12:4 the Bible uses the illustration of the body. It has many parts with different jobs, but all work together, don't they?

There is a certain type of plant our family has grown that shows something very unusual. We are used to plants that you can touch, move, and even transplant without any noticeable effect. But this plant reacts when it is even brushed against lightly. Its leaves fold up and pull back, just like it is saying, "Don't touch me, be careful!" This plant is called the "sensitive plant." Some people are like that plant. They have been hurt many times and even a slight touch or word can cause them pain and a sad reaction. Should we avoid them? No, just like the plants, they need to be cared for, you just have to be extremely careful. How did Jesus treat the people He came in contact with? Matthew 9:36 says that "he was moved with compassion." He cares for everyone.

Look Out for Counterfeits!

Have you ever read or heard of the parable of the wheat and tares? For most people, it is something in the Bible that they don't really understand. This is why God wants us to live in the country and grow gardens. Then we will understand more of what is written in His Word. Jesus studied the book of nature so that He could find lessons to share with the people who followed Him.

When a plot of ground is sown in wheat, it must be watched carefully for weeds. Any weeds should be pulled out before they multiply and rob the wheat of the needed food and water. But there are a group of weeds that are really hard to notice. Most weeds look different than the plant you are growing. But then there are the tares. They are weeds, but they look like the wheat until harvest time. They grow like the wheat, but their roots take away that which is needed by the real wheat plants.

> **WE MUST STUDY THE TRUE PLANT VERY, VERY CAREFULLY, AND THEN WHEN SOMETHING ELSE GROWS BESIDE IT WE KNOW WHETHER IT IS THE REAL PLANT OR A WEED.**

I have noticed in growing carrots that there are wild carrots. In growing oats, there are wild oats; in growing beans, there is a counterfeit; in growing grass, there is a deceiver. What can we do? We must study the true plant very, very carefully, and then when something else grows beside it we know whether it is the real plant or a weed. Jesus warned us about a similar situation in Matthew 13:25–30. What did He tell us would happen?

But while men slept, his enemy came and sowed tares among the wheat, and went his way. But when the blade was sprung up, and brought forth fruit, then appeared the tares also. So the servants of the householder came and said unto him, Sir, didst not thou sow good seed in thy field? from whence then hath it tares? He said unto them, An enemy hath done this. The servants said unto him, Wilt thou then that we go and gather them up? But he said, Nay; lest while ye gather up the tares, ye root up also the wheat with them. Let both grow together until the harvest: and in the time of harvest I will say to the reapers, Gather ye together first the tares, and bind them in bundles to burn them: but gather the wheat into my barn.

How can we tell the difference between true and false things? There are tests that the Bible gives, but we are also told that some things we just have to leave and God will take care of them. Below are some Bible verses that tell us some of the things we need to watch for in our own lives and around us.

Little children, let no man deceive you: he that doeth righteousness is righteous, even as he is righteous. He that committeth sin is of the devil; for the devil sinneth from the beginning. For this purpose the Son of God was manifested, that he might destroy the works of the devil. (1 John 3:7, 8)

Beware of false prophets, which come to you in sheep's clothing, but inwardly they are ravening wolves. Ye shall know them by their fruits. Do men gather grapes of thorns, or figs of thistles? Even so every good tree bringeth forth good fruit; but a corrupt tree bringeth forth evil fruit. A good tree cannot bring forth evil fruit, neither can a corrupt tree bring forth good fruit. Every tree that bringeth not forth good fruit is hewn down, and cast into the fire. Wherefore by their fruits ye shall know them. (Matt. 7:15–20)

What kind of fruit am I bearing? What about you? We can ask the Lord to help us to be true and faithful for Him. Do you remember the story of Ananias and Sapphira? They looked and talked like true Christians, but God knew their hearts. When many other disciples of Jesus were giving money and property to help others, Ananias and Sapphira pretended to give all of the money from the sale of a property, but secretly they held some back. The Holy Spirit knew the truth, and they died because of lying to Him. We must be careful, shouldn't we?

Apply It!

1. Have you had a time to practice being unselfish this week?
2. What unique people did you meet with this week? Can you understand why God made each of us differently?
3. Are you a "sensitive plant" or are you a sturdy plant, growing so that you can help others?
4. Were you truthful in all that you said and did this week? If not, you can ask the Lord to change you to be more like Him.

Chapter 13
Taught by a Fish

"But he that shall endure unto the end, the same shall be saved."
Matthew 24:13

There are so many creatures that teach great lessons, but this one really impressed me. I had read the account of salmon going on long treks to spawn their eggs, but only recently did I have the pleasure of seeing this wonderful creature and its feats of strength.

Near our home the salmon come to where they were born in order to lay eggs. The salmon must travel hundreds of miles, sometimes taking up to six months to travel, usually without eating. This in itself would take lots of perseverance, but this is not the hardest part of the journey. Sometimes the salmon must go up, yes, I said, "up" waterfalls and across rocky areas before they reach their home. Sometimes they have to also fight with predators.

At the place where we observed the salmon, we could see hundreds that had died just before the final stretch. What a sad sight! Having gone so far, so long, they didn't get to the end.

We are also on a journey, heading to heaven. So what should we remember about our journey? Matthew 24:13 reads, "But he that shall endure unto the end, the same shall be saved." We need to endure or *persevere*!

That means to keep on going when we want to give up.

Although some died, there were many salmon that finished their journey. They gathered at the bottom of a manmade waterfall that had a salmon ladder to the side. It was a cement ramp that was quite steep but had steps that went to the top of the dam. Now, if it had just been the ramp that had a trickle of water coming over it that wouldn't be too hard for those determined salmon, but that was not the case. There was a great volume of rushing water coming down the ladder, causing swirling and a lot of pressure against the fish.

Over and over the salmon would try to jump up the steps of the ladder. Many times they would be pushed and thrown against the sides or worse yet, cast down to the bottom again. I couldn't believe how often the fish tried again and again to make it to the top. Just beyond the gate at the top of the ladder was a calm and tranquil pond of water—their home.

> *We need to endure or persevere! That means to keep on going when we want to give up.*

What goal should we be striving for? Philippians 3:12–14 tells us: "Not as though I had already attained, either were already perfect: but I follow after, if that I may apprehend that for which also I am apprehended of Christ Jesus. Brethren, I count not myself to have apprehended: but this one thing I do, forgetting those things which are behind, and reaching forth unto those things which are before, I press toward the mark for the prize of the high calling of God in Christ Jesus." Our goal is to reach what Christ wants for us!

We stood there for one hour. Hundreds of salmon tried, yet we only saw four make it up the ladder to the pond. What a lesson! I left praying that God would help me to be brave and determined enough to go through any obstacle in order to gain heaven.

There is another very serious verse that should challenge us to be very close to Jesus. Matthew 22:14 tells us that "many are called, but few are chosen." What does this tell us? Jesus loves everyone, but we have an enemy who tries to stop us. The only way to make it is to fight against the enemy and ask Jesus to take us to the end. We will have to put forth effort, but He will give us the strength if we really want it and earnestly ask for it.

Many More

Why do the salmon go through all this trouble? To multiply. We have a similar precious privilege on our journey. We can go and tell others.

What is our God-given commission? Let's read Mark 5:19 and 16:15.

Howbeit Jesus suffered him not, but saith unto him, Go home to thy friends, and tell them how great things the Lord hath done for thee, and hath had compassion on thee. (Mark 5:19)

And he said unto them, Go ye into all the world, and preach the gospel to every creature. (Mark 16:15)

As we study God's creatures, we see this same lesson of multiplication repeated, that of survival just to reproduce the species again. Only the salmon have a different fate after they lay their eggs. When the female salmon lays its eggs, she dies and so does the father. They do not receive any reward for their hard work. Their children will hatch and go on a long journey to the ocean, only to repeat the same dangerous trip as their parents.

Not so with the journey to heaven. We can all go! We can receive a wonderful reward, and we can take others with us. We can share the joy and the results. Don't you want to go there? Will you be as determined as the salmon? Think of the wonderful reward that is ahead?

First John 3:2 says, "Beloved, now are we the sons of God, and it doth not yet appear what we shall be: but we know that, when he shall appear, we shall be like him; for we shall see him as he is."

Are you looking forward to seeing Jesus face to face? I am!

Apply It!

1. What should we do when we are tired and ready to give up on something?
2. What is the most important lesson we can learn from the salmon?
3. What is our purpose for living on planet earth?

Chapter 14
Sheep Need Shepherds

"The LORD is my shepherd; I shall not want. He maketh me to lie down in green pastures: he leadeth me beside the still waters."
Psalm 23:1, 2

Have you memorized Psalm 23? It is a favorite passage of Scripture to commit to memory, and it is the theme of this chapter. In Palestine there were many sheep and shepherds that Jesus would have seen as He walked and worked in the countryside. He taught many lessons while using them as an example. It would be exciting if you could go to a farm that has sheep and ask if we could watch them for a while. This makes the lessons more real and special.

Who Is the Shepherd?

This is the question that must be asked and answered first. If you were out in a field with several people and many sheep, how would you determine who is the shepherd? Well, of course, he is the one who takes care of the sheep. The Bible compares us to sheep, so who is our Shepherd? Hebrews 13:20 gives us the answer: "Now the God of peace, that brought again from the dead our Lord Jesus, that great shepherd of the sheep, through the blood of the everlasting covenant."

How does a shepherd feel about his sheep? He cares for them and has compassion for them. He wants to protect them from danger and make sure they have good food to eat and are warm and healthy. A caring shepherd will do whatever it takes to make sure they are ok, even if he has to risk his life to help them. When a sheep is lost, the shepherd needs to find it. Have you ever thought about Jesus searching for us like a shepherd searches for a lost sheep?

"For the Son of man is come to seek and to save that which was lost" (Luke 19:10). It seems that a lost sheep (person) never finds its way back home without the help of the Shepherd. If he stays lost, he will die. What a wonderful picture of Jesus, our loving shepherd, who goes looking for lost and straying sheep like me.

I have noticed that the owner of a piece of property or of livestock seems to care more about what he owns than someone who is hired to care for them. Have you noticed that? Jesus knew this truth as well. That's why he warned about a good shepherd and a hireling, someone who is hired to help with the sheep. When danger comes, the hireling often runs away, but not the shepherd. He is willing to fight against even wolves (John 10:11–14).

I am thankful that Jesus is the shepherd and that He cares so much that He is willing to fight for His sheep. Are you following the Shepherd? Do you know His voice?

For he is our God; and we are the people of his pasture, and the sheep of his hand. To day if ye will hear his voice. (Ps. 95:7)

*Know ye that the L*ORD *he is God: it is he that hath made us, and not we ourselves; we are his people, and the sheep of his pasture. (Ps. 100:3)*

SHEEP OR GOAT?

Did you know there is a difference between sheep and goats? If you remember, Jesus often compared the two. Look in Matthew 25:32, 33: "And before him shall be gathered all nations: and he shall separate them one from another, as a shepherd divideth his sheep from the goats: And he shall set the sheep on his right hand, but the goats on the left."

Sheep are known to be followers. They get to know who their master is, and when they hear his voice, guess what they do? They hear and then they follow. This is what Jesus wants us to do with Him. "My sheep hear my voice, and I know them, and they follow me" (John 10:27).

But how can we hear the voice of our Shepherd when there are many voices and many things to do? The Bible tells us that we need to "be still" and "hear His voice" (Ps. 46:10; Heb. 4:7).

We need soft and quiet hearts. Will you listen for the voice of our Great Shepherd?

Almost all creatures in the wild have good hearing so they can listen for danger. But the difference between a goat and a sheep is the response to the voice.

Follow or Fight?

Goats, like sheep, have good ears. Almost all creatures in the wild have good hearing so they can listen for danger. But the difference between a goat and a sheep is the response to the voice. Have you ever watched a goat, or tried to get him to come to you, or attempted to catch him? As soon as you try to get close, they like to go the other way. They can be very playful and sometimes very hard to deal with. They are known to be stubborn, and they don't listen very well at all.

Sheep, however, are calmer, quieter, and easier to work with. Have you ever watched the time of shearing? We had the privilege not long ago. The big, woolly sheep was brought close to the shearer and promptly set on her haunches. In this position she did not struggle but merely sat still and accepted the treatment bestowed upon her.

What an example of submission to circumstances. Does this remind you of any scriptures? Isaiah 53:6, 7 speaks of Jesus being like a sheep being led to the slaughter, willingly going where He was led and not fighting to get away. I was quite surprised to see this very large animal letting herself be placed in an uncomfortable position and sheared without any resistance. What a lesson!

"All we like sheep have gone astray; we have turned every one to his own way; and the Lord hath laid on him the iniquity of us all. He was oppressed, and he was afflicted, yet he opened not his mouth: he is brought as a lamb to the slaughter, and as a sheep before her shearers is dumb, so he openeth not his mouth" (Isa. 53:6, 7).

Jesus was compared to a sheep in that He was quiet, meek, and did not fight what was about to happen to Him. His act of sacrifice was because of His great love for you and me. Isn't He wonderful?

How can we follow the Great Shepherd? Well, when we hear His voice through the Bible or through godly parents and teachers, we have a choice to make. Will we listen and obey, or will we ignore and disobey. When we follow, there are great blessings. Remember the promises in Psalm 23 about the shepherd's care? Which is your favorite?

Needing Green Grass

If you were a lamb or a full-grown sheep, what would you like to eat most? No, it is not treats, or peanut butter sandwiches, or fruit smoothies. They like fresh, sweet, lush grass. Why? Because God made them that way. The grass gives them a supply of what they need to be strong and healthy.

Has God made us different than sheep? Yes, He has. What has He given to us to keep us strong and healthy? Genesis 1:29 shares the original menu in Eden. It was herb bearing seed, so that means grains and fruits and legumes, and later vegetables. These are the best things to make us healthy and strong.

How do sheep find the wonderful grass they need? The shepherd leads them there. When we need something for our physical, mental, or spiritual health, we can ask our loving Shepherd and He will lead us as well. Look at Proverbs 3:5–8. It is one of my favorite passages to remember. "Trust in the Lord with all thine heart; and lean not unto thine own understanding. In all thy ways acknowledge him, and he shall direct thy paths. Be not wise in thine own eyes: fear the Lord, and depart from evil. It shall be health to thy navel, and marrow to thy bones."

We need direction and guidance in our life, and Jesus can supply that for us!

Watch Out for Wolves!

In our study about weeds, we talked about counterfeits or deceivers, something that is pretending to be something it is not. As Jesus spoke about sheep, He also warned about wolves. Now if you were a sheep and you saw a wolf coming toward you, what would you do? You would cry out in sheep talk and run quickly away from the wolf. You would know that wolves don't want to be friends. They want to destroy. So there would be no playing around. Your life would be at risk.

But what if another sheep comes to you—at least you think it is a sheep. The feet look a little different though, and under the woolly coat, you detect a different smell. Even the nose looks a little different. You are suspicious, and after further investigation, you discover that it is a wolf dressed up like a sheep! Do you know what Jesus was warning about? He knew that the greatest danger was not from those we can tell are definitely wrong, but from those who look and act like sheep but are not really following the Shepherd.

How can I tell whether I am a sheep or a wolf? How can I tell whether someone else is a sheep or a wolf? In Matthew 7:16 it states, "Ye shall know them by their fruits!" If you look carefully, you will be able to tell.

Hear is the full passage in Matthew 7: "Beware of false prophets, which come to you in sheep's clothing, but inwardly they are ravening wolves. Ye shall know them by their fruits. Do men gather grapes of thorns, or figs of thistles? Not every one that saith unto me, Lord, Lord, shall enter into the kingdom of heaven; but he that doeth the will of my Father which is in heaven" (verses 15–17).

Jesus is so wonderful. He doesn't leave us unwarned or unprotected. We can call on Him at all times and in all places, and He will protect us. Praise His holy name! Pick a promise for yourself from the following suggestions and write it out. In fact, it would be good to memorize it.

- "The Lord is my strength and my shield; my heart trusted in him, and I am helped: therefore my heart greatly rejoiceth; and with my song will I praise him" (Ps. 28:7).
- "Thou art my hiding place and my shield: I hope in thy word" (Ps. 119:114).
- "Every word of God is pure: he is a shield unto them that put their trust in him" (Prov. 30:5).

I hope we will keep it in our minds that we are sheep, and we have a great and loving Shepherd to guide us continually. Can you think of someone in the Bible who understood this? I think of Jacob. He made a big mistake and had to leave his home and go to a strange country and work very hard. When it was time to leave, he had trouble with his father-in-law, and then he heard that his brother was coming to attack him

with a great army. He prayed and prayed to God, and the Lord protected, guided, and blessed him for many, many years. Read the story yourself in Genesis 28–33. It is very interesting.

Apply It!

1. How does Jesus feel about you, His sheep?
2. How are the goats different from the sheep in following Jesus?
3. Are you meekly following what Jesus asks or are you hard of hearing?
4. How can you tell the difference between a wolf or a sheep?
5. What special promise did you choose and why?

Chapter 15
Watch the Trees Grow

"Herein is my Father glorified, that ye bear much fruit; so shall ye be my disciples."
John 15:8

Do you like trees? Climbing them, sitting under them, walking near them? Many times in Scripture there are references to trees and to vines. Let's see what they represent. Jeremiah 17:7, 8 tells us that we are to be like a tree planted right by the water. What happens there? When a tree is well watered, its leaves are green, it is healthy, and it will produce nice fruit for us to enjoy.

Blessed is the man that trusteth in the Lord, and whose hope the Lord is. For he shall be as a tree planted by the waters, and that spreadeth out her roots by the river, and shall not see when heat cometh, but her leaf shall be green; and shall not be careful in the year of drought, neither shall cease from yielding fruit. (Jer. 17:7, 8)

Water represents Jesus—He quenches our thirst, cleans us, and gives us what we need to grow. He is also light like the sunshine. When we grow beside Him and send our roots deep into His Word, we can grow fruit, the fruit of holiness in our lives.

What about vines? Are they different? Jesus used the example of grapevines. They grow from a main stock and then branch out, holding on to different things to support them and keep them off the ground. Vines usually grow a fruit too. What is the lesson from the vine? John 15:4, 5 tells us that we can be attached to Jesus, the vine, and then He will give us what we need to grow well: "Abide in me, and I in you. As the branch cannot bear fruit of itself, except it abide in the vine; no more can ye, except ye abide in me. I am the vine, ye are the branches: He that abideth in me, and I in him, the same bringeth forth much fruit: for without me ye can do nothing."

> **When we grow beside Him and send our roots deep into His Word, we can grow fruit, the fruit of holiness in our lives.**

Jesus spoke about abiding in the vine. If you have ever tried to graft one branch into a vine or a tree, you will know that the branch must be inserted into the main trunk, secured there in some way so that it will actually grow together and the life from the plant will go into the branch. If it were placed there and then removed, put there again, removed again, placed there again and removed once more, would the branch be able to grow and bear fruit? No. It needs to stay there. So we need to stay connected with Jesus all the time. We also cannot grow by being attached to another branch. We have to be connected with the True Vine—Jesus. We must be connected with Him, not just once a week, but every day, every hour, every minute. This is how the Holy Spirit changes us and helps us to bear the right fruit.

Homes for Others

Plants have many uses. Most of our food comes from plants. Look at everything you ate for breakfast or lunch today and figure out what plant it came from. Aren't you thankful that God gave us growing things? Plants or trees are also used to build things. What products in your home were made from plants or trees?

Did you know that trees also furnish homes for other creatures? Think of how many of God's creation live in the trees. There are insects, birds, raccoons, squirrels, worms, chipmunks, and a host of other creatures that depend on trees to live. If you have a chance, go for a walk in the woods and write down how many different creatures you see in or on the trees.

Can we be a "home" for someone? No, they can't live in us, but we could provide for others what a home provides for us. Maybe we can give food to someone, or protection, or warmth. By helping others we are blessed.

Can you think of a Bible character who was like a tree that bore fruit? I think of Dorcas. She was a woman who had a heart for Jesus and others. She tried to help whoever and wherever she could with clothing,

food, or kind words. When she died, people were so upset. They loved her so much! When Peter arrived he prayed over her body, and God brought her back to life! Wow! I sure would like to have people be so thankful that I am alive. What about you?

Apply It!

1. How do I know I am planted beside Jesus?
2. Have I tried to be a help and blessing to anyone today?
3. What kind of fruit am I showing in my character?

Chapter 16
Water

"And the Spirit and the bride say, Come. And let him that heareth say, Come. And let him that is athirst come. And whosoever will, let him take the water of life freely."
Revelation 22:17

What is so special about water? Can we live without it? Where is its source? How do we get it? The water cycle is very interesting. Let us consider the rain sent from heaven. You feel a few drops fall from the clouds in the sky. If it is warm, you'll probably enjoy it. If cool, you will run for shelter, but have you ever taken the time to appreciate the fact that it is falling?

Only Service

During and after a rainfall, have you noticed what happens with the water that has gathered? It may be absorbed into the soil or if there are large amounts falling at once, or falling on a hard surface, you will notice that the water collects and heads for the lowest place. It may be a small trickle, turning into a streamlet, heading for the nearest creek or stream or ditch. It will run and flow until it reaches a river and onward to a lake or maybe even a sea. Of course, a lot of water seeps deep into the ground, watering the earth and keeping things growing.

Does the water running deeper and deeper into the ground remind you of anything? It reminds me of Philippians 2:5–8, the passage of Scripture that explains how low Jesus was willing to go for you and me. Jesus was willing to take the lowest place, ready to serve, ready to do whatever was necessary to help others.

Let this mind be in you, which was also in Christ Jesus: Who, being in the form of God, thought it not robbery to be equal with God: But made himself of no reputation, and took upon him the form of a servant, and was made in the likeness of men: And being found in fashion as a man, he humbled himself, and became obedient unto death, even the death of the cross. (Phil. 2:5–8)

If we want to be followers of Jesus and if His Holy Spirit lives within our hearts, we will be like the water. We will be willing to serve and go wherever we are needed to help others. Jesus gave this instruction many times by word and by His example.

Then said Jesus unto his disciples, If any man will come after me, let him deny himself, and take up his cross, and follow me. (Matt. 16:24)

"… by love serve one another. For all the law is fulfilled in one word, even in this; Thou shalt love thy neighbor as thyself. (Gal. 5:13, 14)

How did Jesus act as a young person your age? Have you ever thought about that? He was always willing to help and to serve others. He was patient, truthful, obedient to principle, and always courteous. Will you copy Him?

Blessings Abound

Have you noticed what happens along the path of the water? Wherever it goes the vegetation beside it benefits. The next time you are walking beside running water look at what is growing nearby. Water gives life to plants, fish, animals, birds, and even insects along the way. It gives the moisture necessary for things to grow and the means that all can be made clean, even people.

Like water that refreshes everything around it, how can you be a blessing to those around you? We need to remember that the reason we were created was to do good works (Eph. 2:10). So bring all the good you can into your life and bless others with it. I remember reading a poem almost thirty years ago. I do not remember it exactly, but what stuck in my brain for so long is written below. It became a saying to live by. I hope it will for you too.

> **So bring all the good you can into your life and bless others with it.**

*I will pass this way but once
Any good that I may do
Let me do it now
For I will not pass this way again.*

(An abbreviated form of the poem credited to Stephen Grellet)

Wash Me

We have already learned how important water is for quenching thirst. Without water to drink, we would die, for every part of our physical body requires water to live and function efficiently. Water is the principle element needed to transport the other required elements to all the cells of the body and to remove the toxic wastes. Water cleans our insides. What about the outside of our body? Is it important to be clean? As you read Isaiah 52:11 and 1 Corinthians 3:17 you will get the clear idea that we must be clean both inside and out. Remember that defile means to make unclean.

Depart ye, depart ye, go ye out from thence, touch no unclean thing; go ye out of the midst of her; be ye clean, that bear the vessels of the LORD. (Isa. 52:11)

If any man defile the temple of God, him shall God destroy; for the temple of God is holy, which temple ye are. (1 Cor. 3:17)

What happens if we do not take care to have a clean body? We begin to smell bad, and because of a build-up of toxins, we may become sick. Just as we need physical water to clean our bodies, we need spiritual water to cleanse us from spiritual uncleanness caused by wrong thoughts, attitudes, and actions. Who is the only One able to cleanse us from the filth of sin and selfishness? Jesus! As you read Psalm 51, you can especially see how David really wanted to be clean from sin, and he knew the Lord was the one to do the cleaning.

Wash me thoroughly from mine iniquity, and cleanse me from my sin. For I acknowledge my transgressions: and my sin is ever before me. Against thee, thee only, have I sinned, and done this evil in thy sight: that thou mightest be justified when thou speakest, and be clear when thou judgest. Behold, I was shapen in iniquity, and in sin did my mother conceive me. Behold, thou desirest truth in the inward parts: and in the hidden part thou shalt make me to know wisdom. Purge me with hyssop, and I shall be clean: wash me, and I shall be whiter than snow. (Ps. 51:2–7)

Water Has Power!

As you read the Bible, how many times do you read stories about water? Think about the Red Sea, the bitter water, the Jordon River, the river of water coming out of the temple, the well of water, etc. Can you see something spectacular about water? In a small droplet, we do not see much potential, but put hundreds of thousands of millions of droplets together and what do you have? Power! Who is able to harness the power of water? Only God! Do you remember the story of Moses and the Red Sea?

And Moses stretched out his hand over the sea; and the LORD caused the sea to go back by a strong east wind all that night, and made the sea dry land, and the waters were divided. And the children of Israel went into the midst of the sea upon the dry ground: and the waters were a wall unto them on their right hand, and on their left. (Exod. 14:21, 22)

No man could stand against the power of water, but God stopped it for the sake of protecting His children. This is to teach us the greater lesson of what God's living water can do in our lives.

Do you have problems and troubles, things you cannot understand? God's power is available. It is good to memorize Jeremiah 32:17 so that whenever we face a big challenge, we will be reminded of God's power: "Ah Lord God! behold, thou hast made the heaven and the earth by thy great power and stretched out arm, and there is nothing too hard for thee."

Even as God sets the boundaries of water, so He allows only those things that we can handle by His help and strength. When we face something that seems too hard and too big and too painful, we need to remember that God promises help, strength, and a way out (1 Cor. 10:13). I am so glad we can trust Him.

Lifted Up

Water droplets travel a great distance before they land on your head. Before they gathered into clouds, a process of evaporation occurred. Those little bits of moisture had to be lifted from the earth. What does this teach? Keep reading.

There is moisture in the soil that, when warmed by the sunshine, invisibly rises into the sky. There are also large and small bodies of water where the same process occurs.

In the same way, when Jesus, the Sun of righteousness (Mal. 4:2), warms our hearts, we are lifted up, or raised up into heavenly places, meaning that our thoughts are focused on Jesus and not the things on earth. In this way, we can be a blessing to others because our life is not about what we want but it is about serving Him and blessing others.

Can you think of some good works that would be done by someone who has the love of Jesus in his or her heart? There could be many different things like making up the bed for your parents or brother or sister, doing the dishes, helping someone with homework, making a card to encourage someone, helping someone with their garden, etc. There are hundreds and maybe thousands of ways that we can bless others.

I am reminded of Naaman's servant girl. We don't know much about her except that her faithful work and kind words made a huge difference in Naaman's life. He was sick with leprosy and destined to be separated from his family, his friends, and his job, but her example and suggestion that he go to the prophet of Israel resulted in his healing. So enjoy being a blessing not just today, but every day!

Apply It!

1. Have you felt the warmth of Jesus' love in your heart today?
2. How were you able to help someone this week?
3. What kind things could be done this Sabbath to help someone else?
4. What did you learn about being clean for Jesus?
5. Have you asked God to use His power to help you in your life today?

Epilogue
More Thoughts

I hope you are getting the idea of how to learn from and teach from God's book of nature. The lessons will never end, so you can begin your own collection.

If you would like activities to go along with some of these lessons, you will find them in the next section.

May the Lord richly bless and guide you in your learning.

PJ Stemmler

Appendix
Activities Section

This section is designed to use with the book, ***Nature Speaks—Are We Listening?*** You can use these activities for Bible lessons, children or youth programs, Sabbath school, or any other time you want to teach children Bible truths through nature. A few ideas are listed here, which will hopefully help you spark other ideas of your own. Remember two things: adapt to the ages of your students and enjoy the process.

Each section has the following components:

- Theme/focus
- Memory verse
- Song
- Bible story options that teach the same theme/focus
- Suggested inside craft activities and the needed supplies
- Suggested outside activities and the needed supplies

I trust you will find this helpful in your quest to learn and teach from the book of nature.

Ants

Theme/Focus: Diligence in working together, being small yet mighty

Memory Verse: "Go to the ant, thou sluggard; consider her ways, and be wise: Which having no guide, overseer, or ruler, Provideth her meat in the summer, and gathereth her food in the harvest" (Prov. 6:6–8)

Song: "Work for the Night Is Coming"

Bible Story Options:
- Nehemiah rebuilding the wall of Jerusalem (Neh. 1–13)
- Building the sanctuary with the offerings and abilities God gave (Exod. 25:8; 36)
- The disciples and what they accomplished in the book of Acts (use chapters 1 and 2, or any other)

Nature Talk: Ants are small but helpful, diligent, and mighty to accomplish what they need to.

Inside Activity Options:
- Label and color a picture of an ant
- Have everyone try to pick up something proportionately as large as an ant carries. For example, if an ant can carry something ten times its weight, try to figure out the weight of each person and then find the weight of something ten times heavier. Do not allow anyone to hurt themselves while trying to lift the object.
- Make a list of projects that could be done together that would help each other.
- Make a people chain like the ant chains.

Needed Supplies:
- Picture(s) to color
- Crayons, colored pencils, or paint

Outside Activity Options:
- Go on a string search or micro hike. For the string search, take a piece of string and lay it on the ground in a circle. Create the same size circle for each child. Give an allotted period of time for the children to study their little circle, searching for what creatures are there and what they are doing. A micro hike is similar. A very short distance or space is allotted for students to find the little creatures that are dwelling and working nearby. Pens and notebooks would be good for older ones. Allow for time to share what they found.
- Find an anthill. Do not destroy or disturb it, but watch and see how diligent the ants are in their work. It may be interesting to try to follow one ant and see how far it goes. Laying some crumb bait at a distance can help keep some control on how far students wander to watch the process.

Needed Supplies:
- Pieces of string, about three feet long
- Notebook and pen or pencil to write down what you see

BEES

Theme/Focus: Working together

Memory Verse: "They helped every one his neighbor; and every one said to his brother, Be of good courage" (Isa. 41:6)

Song: "O Brother Be Faithful"

Bible Story Option: The story of Deborah (which means bee) helping Barak

Nature Talk: Be faithful to your tasks and helping each other for the good of the whole

Inside Activity Options:
- Explain where honey comes from, and share other interesting facts about bees. Honey is actually nectar that is collected, stored in a special compartment in the bee, taken to the hive and dehydrated somewhat, then sealed to be used later.
- Label and color a picture of a bee and maybe the hive too.
- Identify where a bee is born and how they must take care to clean the hive or disease will set in and hurt the whole hive.
- Have a beekeeper bring in an observation hive and other interesting beekeeper paraphernalia.
- Make a list of products made by bees and why bees are so important in food production.

Needed Supplies:
- Pictures to label and color
- Posters or media form to see the bees in action
- Honey, pollen, wax, maybe lotion, shoe protection, something baked with honey
- Bee equipment

Outside Activity Options:
- Visit a beehive (with proper protection)
- Go for a walk and look for bees and other pollinators doing their job of collecting nectar, pollinating plants, and maybe even giving directions to others.
- Give each student an allotted task, just like the bees have in the hive. A certain space will be the designated "hive." Some will be nurse bees, some repair bees, some giving directions to where the food is, some foragers, looking for nectar sources, some guard bees so enemies don't come in. Have something collectible that they can bring into the hive and enjoy together later.

Needed Supplies:
- A group project such as weeding, bringing in firewood, shoveling snow for neighbors, raking leaves, picking up groceries for a shut-in, etc.
- Protective clothing such as a bug screen hat, long sleeves, pants, and gloves. Check to see if any are known to have an allergy to bee stings. Remind everyone that to keep calm and quiet is the best protection. Light colors are best too.
- Don't wear anything fragrant or smelly. Bees can become irritated with such things as perfumes, colognes, shampoos, hydraulic oil, diesel fuel, etc.

BIRDS

Theme/Focus: Realizing your value to God brings cheerfulness and singing

Memory Verse: "Fear ye not therefore, ye are of more value than many sparrows" (Matt. 10:31).

Song: "His Eye Is on the Sparrow" or "God Loves the Little Sparrow"

Bible Story Options:
- Jesus teaches about sparrows (Matt. 10:31)
- Each one is so valuable that Jesus would have died just for one, example of Mary Magdalene (Matt. 26:1–13; Luke 7:36–50)

Nature Talk: Birds love to sing, especially early in the morning. They are happy and content. Each kind is different.

Inside Activity Options:
- Bird identification papers to sort according to type. There are many varieties that can be sorted into groups. A good bird guide will be helpful. Show the different types of nests, beaks, and habitats.
- Coloring and labeling bird parts
- Nest building
- Make a list of all the things you can be thankful for and then sing a song of praise and thanksgiving to God.

Needed Supplies:
- A good bird identification book
- Coloring pages of birds at a realistic size so that they could be placed on a stick if desired
- Scissors, tape, glue sticks, or string to make a mobile
- Sticks, straw, clay or glue, newspaper, and aprons for making nests. You may want to do this one outside. You could try making a large nest for an eagle or a small sparrow's nest.

Outside Activity Options:
- Put your colored bird on a stick and hide yourself behind a bush, being very quiet to see if another bird will come close. It is important to stay quiet and remain still for quite a long time. (This is an excellent exercise for stillness.)
- Listen for their distinctive calls and try to tell which is which
- Rise early to see who's up when; this can be shared the next day or given as an exercise to older students the day of this particular program
- Find discarded, unused nests

Needed Supplies:
- Bird sticks
- Blanket to sit on
- Binoculars
- Notebook and writing utensils.

Butterflies

Theme/Focus: Metamorphosis—we can be changed into something beautiful!

Memory Verse: "Therefore if any man be in Christ, he is a new creature: old things are passed away; behold, all things are become new" (2 Cor. 5:17).

Song: "Live Out Thy Life Within Me"; "Praise Him, Praise Him, Jesus Our Blessed Redeemer"

Bible Story Options:
- The transformation of John from one of the sons of thunder to John the writer of love; story of he and James and their desire to call down fire on the village versus his main theme in the books by his name (Mark 3:17; Luke 9:54, 55; 1 John)
- The miraculous healing of the demoniac who was transformed into his right mind (Mark 5)

Nature Talk: Caterpillar to chrysalis to butterfly. What else changes forms?

Inside Activity Options:
- Identification of different types of butterflies and/or moths
- Identify what they eat and where they live; migration is also very interesting
- Identification and labeling of the different stages of development
- Use felt or paper and create your own caterpillars and butterflies, matching real patterns; can be made into a mobile or window hanger

Needed Supplies:
- Pre-cut felt or paper pieces (tissue paper is nice for butterflies)
- Glue, pipe cleaners
- Photocopied pictures to label and color

Outside Activity Options:
- Going on a butterfly hunt to see how many different ones can be found (be very careful not to hurt any)
- Hunting for plants or flowers that butterflies would look for and why, or look for signs of caterpillars
- Looking for other things that change in their development

Needed Supplies:
- Binoculars
- Butterfly nets (only if the student is old enough to use it wisely)
- Insect field guide
- Bug detention cage (let insects go after observation)
- Notebook and pencil

Deer

Theme/Focus: Listening very carefully

Memory Verses:
- "As the hart panteth after the water brooks, so panteth my soul after thee, O God" (Ps. 42:1).
- "And thine ears shall hear a word behind thee, saying, This is the way, walk ye in it, when ye turn to the right hand, and when ye turn to the left" (Isa. 30:21).

Song: "As the Deer"

Bible Story Options:
- Joseph was given dreams in order to protect the baby Jesus from harm (Matt. 2:13, 19)
- Peter called to visit Cornelius (Acts 10)

Nature Talk: Listening for danger and instruction

Inside Activity Options:
- Picture of a deer to color—discuss that the color changes with the seasons
- Plan a camouflage session with either blankets or clothing of differing colors for different areas
- Identify deer prints, male or female or baby
- Identify antlers and discuss their use
- Identify and discuss what deer eat

Needed Supplies:
- Pre-printed pictures
- Pictures of deer in different seasons
- Deer prints
- An antler
- Samples of deer food
- Camouflage clothing or blankets

Outside Activity Options:
- Deer print hunt; make a mold or replica of a deer print as an example of what to search for
- Camouflage hide-n-seek
- Scavenger hunt to find a deer path
- Set up a feeding station for the deer (away from your garden)

Needed Supplies:
- Plaster to make a deer print mold
- Camouflage clothing or blankets
- Feeding station stand

FISH (SALMON)

Theme/Focus: Perseverance! What is it? How do I develop it?

Memory Verses:
- "Behold, we count them happy which endure" (James 5:11).
- "My brethren, count it all joy when ye fall into divers temptations; Knowing this, that the trying of your faith worketh patience. But let patience have her perfect work, that ye may be perfect and entire, wanting nothing" (James 1:2–4).

Song: "I Will Follow Thee My Saviour"; "O Brother Be Faithful"

Bible Story Options:
- Jonah caught by a fish. He had to persevere in prayer.
- Jesus in the wilderness of temptation, then in the garden. He chose His Father's will no matter how difficult it was (Matt. 4; Mark 14).

Nature Talk: How the salmon and many other creatures must persevere to survive.

Inside Activity Options:
- Color a picture of the salmon in varying stages of its life
- Show on a map the distance that a salmon may sometimes travel
- Show a video clip of how much this creature must persevere to get to its goal
- Make a list of things that we must persevere at

Needed Supplies:
- Pre-printed pictures
- Map
- Video clip
- Practice sessions on perseverance

Outside Activity Options:
- Locate a body of water where fish are and carefully view them. If you can see salmon, wonderful, but they are not usually found locally.
- Visit a waterfall or salmon ladder
- Create a type of fish ladder for your students. It will need to be something challenging but not dangerous. Without the danger element, the challenge may be in repetition. Example: Go up this ladder 25 times and see how you feel. :)

Needed Supplies:
- Location to visit
- Fish ladder for people

FLOWERS

Theme/Focus: Grow where you are.

Memory Verse: "Consider the lilies how they grow: they toil not, they spin not; and yet I say unto you, that Solomon in all his glory was not arrayed like one of these. If then God so clothe the grass, which is to day in the field, and to morrow is cast into the oven; how much more will he clothe you, O ye of little faith?" (Luke 12:27, 28)

Song: "This is My Father's World"

Bible Story Option: Joseph went through many challenges but chose to be faithful wherever he was planted (Gen. 37–45)

Nature Talk: Flowers grow and share their beauty and fragrance no matter where they are planted.

Inside Activity Options:
- Discuss what is needed for flowers to grow—God's tools are sunshine, water, and soil
- Discuss the pollination process and how flowers grow into fruit
- Label and color pictures of different types of flowers
- Identify edible flowers
- Plant flowers in a pot or create a dried flower arrangement
- Use a magnifying glass to examine God's creation closer
- Cut and paste pictures to make a poster about God's goodness
- Make bookmarks or cards from pressed flowers

Needed Supplies:
- Pre-printed pictures, coloring tools, scissors, glue, card stock paper and laminate material for bookmarks
- Dried, pressed flowers
- Samples of real flowers
- Flower pots, soil, small shovels or spoons, plants, or seeds
- Marker and stir sticks to label pots
- Magnifying glass

Outside Activity Options:
- Plant identification walk
- Plant some flowers in a garden (use a variety of color)
- Do a plant-sniffing walk and figure out the one you like best
- Gather some flowers (with permission) for pressing and drying
- Find some edible flowers and use them at lunch
- Build a new flowerbed from scratch, include the following steps: proper preparation, stone and weed removal, planning, amending, and planting
- Create a living flower arrangement to take to someone

Needed Supplies:
- Prepared flowerbed or location to add a flowerbed
- Either seed or potted plants to transplant and markers to identify type
- Edible plant guide
- Location(s) to visit to do your identification and sniff walks

FOREST CREATURES

Theme/Focus: Each one is unique. All are important.

Memory Verses:
- "And God made the beast of the earth after his kind, and cattle after their kind, and every thing that creepeth upon the earth after his kind: and God saw that it was good" (Gen. 1:25)
- "Let them praise the name of the LORD: for he commanded, and they were created … Beasts, and all cattle; creeping things, and flying fowl" (Ps. 148:5, 10).

Song: "How Great Thou Art"; "Praise Ye the Lord"

Bible Story Option: The choosing of twelve disciples with very different character traits and positions in life

Nature Talk: How forest creatures differ in their characteristics and how they warn others

Inside Activity Options:
- Coloring pages of a raccoon, skunk, or porcupine
- Touch and feel experiment of sharp or prickly objects
- Craft project to make a porcupine
- Smell experiment of bad odors

Needed Supplies:
- Pre-printed pictures or blank pages with drawing or coloring tools
- Research books and/or field guides to forest creatures
- A list of animals that live near you
- Examples of sharp things or smelly things

Outside Activity Options:
- Going for a creature hunt in the daytime
- Looking for habitats, prints, and telltale signs of forest creatures

Needed Supplies:
- Binoculars and field guide
- Map to follow and plot findings on
- Notebook to keep track of things
- Blanket and water (it might take awhile)

Rocks

Theme/Focus: Unchangeable

Memory Verse: "For who is God save the Lord? or who is a rock save our God?" (Ps. 18:31)

Song: "The Lord is Our Rock, in Him We Hide"

Bible Story Option: The wise man who built his house on the Rock (Matt. 7)

Nature Talk: Showing through rocks that we can be steadfast in principle, unmoved by circumstances. A secondary lesson shows that some rocks, although rough on the outside, are actually quite beautiful within.

Inside Activity Options:
- Look at different types and sizes of rocks
- Identify different uses of rocks
- Look at pictures of hidden gems
- Polish a rock
- Mount a rock on wood and write a lesson learned
- Write one word that reminds you about God on a rock with a marker

Needed Supplies:
- A book about rocks
- Samples of various rocks
- Pieces of wood and cement (to compare rock with)
- Pictures of gems
- Polished rocks
- Glue or other items if mounting a stone
- Permanent markers

Outside Activity Options:
- Go for a rock hunt
- Try to find gems inside of rocks
- Make a pile of rocks for a flowerbed
- Find other uses for rocks

Needed Supplies:
- Pre-determined path to find examples of rocks—hide some special stones or rocks ahead of time

SHEEP

Theme/Focus: Following the right leader

Memory Verse: "Know ye that the Lord he is God: it is he that hath made us, and not we ourselves; we are his people, and the sheep of his pasture" (Ps. 100:3).

Song: "I Will Follow Thee My Saviour"

Bible Story Options: The lost sheep (Luke 15)

Nature Talk: Following the Shepherd with the right attitude

Inside Activity Options:
- Make cotton ball sheep
- List times we need to follow the right leader
- Play follow the leader for young children
- Discuss following cheerfully and being content with what God allows in our lives
- Discuss things that need to be changed so that we can be a sheep and not a goat
- Examine what sheep eat and how it affects their disposition

Needed Supplies:
- Paper, glue, and cotton balls
- Pre-printed pictures
- Facts about sheep
- Pre-determined activities to practice following instructions
- Examples of sheep food

Outside Activity Options:
- Look for good places that sheep would pasture
- Visit a sheep farm and if possible watch them shear a sheep
- Play follow the leader along a long path; practice calling out directions to see if the sheep will recognize your voice and follow your instructions

Needed Supplies:
- A farm to visit sheep
- A watering hole or pasture to visit

HEAVENS

Theme/Focus: The heavens declare the glory of God, teaching what He is like

Memory Verse: "The heavens declare the glory of God; and firmament showeth His handiwork" (Ps. 19:1)

Song: "Great and Marvellous Are Thy Works"

Bible Story Option: The wise men following the star to see Jesus

Nature Talk: The wonder and majesty of what is in the heavens

Inside Activity Options:
- Make a model constellation using black paper and a hole punch
- Make a list of what is in the heavens
- Make a model of the sun, moon, stars, and other planets
- Give each student a position to rotate around the sun
- Create light and dark spaces (representing the sun and moon), or use blindfolds and ask students to go places and do things
- Show an example of a plant that has been in the light versus one that has been in the dark

Needed Supplies:
- Black construction paper
- Hole punch
- String to hang the model
- Constellation patterns
- Blindfolds
- Flashlights and a dark place
- A plant that hasn't had light and one that has

Outside Activity Options:
- Go for a night walk
- Make a storm (use a sprinkling can or hose, a high speed fan, a dark space, etc.)
- Look at what grows in the dark versus what grows in the light
- Visit someone who has a telescope to view the heavens
- Visit somewhere that moon position is shown in the tides
- Make a simple sundial (paint an inverted paper plate, then stick the pain brush through the center; place the sundial in a sunny place and make a mark every hour based on where the shadow of the paint brush falls on the plate)

Needed Supplies:
- Pre-determined locations to find the examples needed
- Paper plates, paint, and a paint brush

TREES

Theme/Focus: Growing to be useful

Memory Verse: "Blessed is the man that walketh not in the counsel of the ungodly, nor standeth in the way of sinners, nor sitteth in the seat of the scornful. But his delight is in the law of the Lord; and in his law doth he meditate day and night. And he shall be like a tree planted by the rivers of water, that bringeth forth his fruit in his season; his leaf also shall not wither; and whatsoever he doeth shall prosper" (Ps. 1:1–3).

Song: "Brighten the Corner Where You Are"

Bible Story Options:
- The fig tree that didn't bear fruit (Luke 13)
- The examples of trees used for really special things like the building of the sanctuary (Exodus), the cedars of Lebanon to build Solomon's temple (2 Chronicles), and the tree that Jesus hung on to die for us (Acts 5:30).

Nature Talk: Trees grow from something very small to be used for good and important purposes.

Inside Activity Options:
- Discuss and show examples of the small seeds that large trees grow from; label the various seeds
- Examine how to tell the age of a tree
- Find what types of trees grow in your area
- Discuss the different stages of growth (a young tree has soft bark and is therefore more flexible; an older one has deeper roots, harder bark, and tends to be more steadfast)
- Discuss and find pictures of the uses of trees or their byproducts
- Color and label the parts of the tree
- Tree identification puzzle; copy pictures and guess what kind
- Mount leaf and bark samples on poster board and label
- Paint a picture of a tree that you really like
- Make an indoor tree

Needed Supplies:
- Tree identification book
- Paper, paint, aprons, construction paper, pens, or markers
- Branch and leaf samples
- Setup large branches to make your own indoor tree; hang pressed, waxed leaves on the branches
- Pictures to label and color

Outside Activity Options:
- Tree identification walk; gather seed or guess its type by its fruit
- Guess the age of a tree by the branches and the root ball size
- Discover what lives in the trees
- Look at things made from wood
- Plant a tree from seed or a young transplant

Needed Supplies:
- Tape measure, magnifying glass, and notebook
- Tree identification book
- Containers to collect seeds

WATER

Theme/Focus: Cleanliness and giving

Memory Verse: "And he said unto me, It is done. I am Alpha and Omega, the beginning and the end. I will give unto him that is athirst of the fountain of the water of life freely" (Rev. 21:6).

Song: "Create in Me a Clean Heart"

Bible Story Option: The woman at the well

Nature Talk: The properties of water to clean and to give life

Inside Activity Options:
- Feel it, drink it, freeze it, steam it
- Make a water intake record
- Go for a walk and then draw a picture of what water you found
- Write a poem about water
- Demonstrate how to be clean and the consequences of being dirty
- Demonstrate how clean water would be if it is strained through a dirty filter
- Demonstrate the blessings of water to animal, plant, birds, people, and even insects

Needed Supplies:
- Water, heating element, ice cubes, and containers for water
- Paper and markers
- Toothbrush, wash cloth, basin
- Water pitcher, straining cloth, muddy water, clean water
- Watering can

Outside Activity Options:
- Water walk; go looking for places that water is or has been
- Look for creatures that live in water
- Clean up a trail or waterway
- Record the blessings you see from the water along your walk
- Build or create a watering place for small creatures or birds

Needed Supplies:
- A trail or waterway
- Container to look at collected water
- Magnifying glass
- Field guide for ponds and streams

We invite you to view the complete
selection of titles we publish at:

www.TEACHServices.com

Scan with your mobile
device to go directly
to our website.

Please write or email us your praises, reactions, or
thoughts about this or any other book we publish at:

P.O. Box 954
Ringgold, GA 30736

info@TEACHServices.com

TEACH Services, Inc., titles may be purchased in bulk for
educational, business, fund-raising, or sales promotional use.
For information, please e-mail:

BulkSales@TEACHServices.com

Finally, if you are interested in seeing
your own book in print, please contact us at

publishing@TEACHServices.com

We would be happy to review your manuscript for free.

www.ingramcontent.com/pod-product-compliance
Lightning Source LLC
Chambersburg PA
CBHW060923170426
43192CB00021B/2858